SOUTH COUN

True Tales

of

Lust & Love

True Tales
of
Lust & Love

EDITED BY
ANNA DAVID

Soft Skull Press
an imprint of Counterpoint

Library of Congress Cataloging-in-Publication Data is available.

ISBN 978-1-59376-538-5

Cover design by Jen Heuer
Interior design by Sabrina Plomitallo-González,
Neuwirth & Associates

Soft Skull Press
An Imprint of COUNTERPOINT
1919 Fifth Street
Berkeley, CA 94710
www.softskull.com

Printed in the United States of America
Distributed by Publishers Group West

10 9 8 7 6 5 4 3 2 1

For the men who inspired these tales,
and the women who could grow from them

Table of Contents

Dating

Love—or Something Like It

True Tales
of
Lust & Love

Foreword

A few—possibly too many—years ago, I cowrote a popular relationship book for women called *He's Just Not That Into You*. When people asked me why I—a TV writer and comedian—felt I had the right to write about relationships, and specifically about how women should handle their affairs with disinterested men, my answer was always the same.

"Because I like women," I would say. I mean, I love them, too, but first and foremost, I really, really like them.

As a young dude, I would always think, during BB gun wars with my friends, "Why aren't we where the girls are?" Not that recreating Vietnam in Ken Flax's backyard wasn't a blast—it was, I swear—but in the back of my mind, or sometimes even in the front, a recurring thought would be there. And it would be something along the lines of: *Seriously dudes, this is bullshit.*

I always loved being in the company of girls, not just because they were awesome to look at and smelled like candy but because I loved listening to them talk, crack up—hell, I even liked to watch them eat. I loved trying to figure out everything I could about them. I was genuinely fascinated by what made them giggle and what made them sad, why they liked certain boys and not others, what their lives were like and if they ever thought about me. The point is that, for my money, you can do no better than to be in the unguarded company of women—whether you're a woman or a man.

That is the intrinsic beauty of this book. It allows you to hang out with a group of smart, funny, dirty, vulnerable, independent, neurotic, capable, and adventurous women. The fact that all of them have opened their hearts and lives to the rest of us feels like a gift—a reward for all that hard work I put into those BB gun wars of my youth. And so I say this awesome collection of personal essays should be essential reading for all women trying to navigate the murky waters of lust and love—and for any man hoping to swim alongside them.

Okay, time for the man to shut up and let the women talk.

—Greg Behrendt,
coauthor of *He's Just Not That Into You*

Introduction

To say that the storytelling show I put on every month in L.A. inspired this book would be like saying that chocolate inspired my love for candy. Nearly all of the stories collected here have been told at the live show, with only essays by a few of my favorite non-L.A.-dwelling writers rounding out the pack—which is to say that all of these essays *would* have been told at the show had some of those who penned them not been three thousand or so miles away. It is also to say that I consider chocolate a necessity after every meal—including breakfast.

I didn't mean to create a storytelling show. I had barely ever even been to a storytelling show. But in October of 2011, when my memoir, *Falling for Me*, was published, after I'd done just one reading at a local bookstore in

L.A., the publicist I was working with told me that she couldn't get me any more bookstore readings. In L.A., she explained, there are so many celebrities with books coming out that the major bookstores pretty much wanted to book just them.

I did not take this news well.

I had spent years living my life, then several more years writing about living my life, so one measly reading in the city I loved and lived in would not suffice.

Then I had a new thought: even when you *do* manage to land a reading at a bookstore, it's tough to get people to show up. As someone who doesn't always want to go to other people's readings, I understand this: who wants to battle rush hour to sit and listen to a friend read aloud a book that may well be dull? Anyone who's ever been taken hostage at a reading by an enthusiastic author who goes on for an hour straight knows this can be a high-risk activity. And then there's the fact that, as a friend and supporter, you feel all this pressure to spend the $24.95 or whatever it is buying the book—a pressure that I can assure you is real because we, the authors, are putting it on you. And we are putting it on you because we feel, whether it's true or not, that our book publishers are putting it on us. In other words, sure, it's great that you showed up but we really, really want you to buy the book.

So then I had a brainstorm and it went like this:

people may not like to go to readings, but they sure do like to go to storytelling shows. Even my extremely unscientific, unintentional survey of our culture had left me with the knowledge that storytelling had become a "thing." In addition, people like attractive women and they also like to laugh. And I knew from my years as the sex, dating, and relationship expert on G4's *Attack of the Show!* (and from, well, living in the world) that people also enjoy stories about sex, love, and dating. I did some calculations in my head and out came the equation that I should call my reading a storytelling show focused on lust and love and invite the funniest women I could find to join me.

This means that in January of 2012, I put on what I thought would be a onetime extravaganza. I got to read my memoir aloud and some other women—comedian and writer friends—told their tales of dating, reuniting with exes, rejection, and the like. And no thanks to me—I'm pretty sure I was the weakest link there—True Tales of Lust & Love was an instant hit; as it turns out, if you call a reading a storytelling show and invite a bunch of other funny and fierce ladies to participate, people will not only show up but they'll also wait in line and pay good money for the experience. But even more remarkable than the crowd was, for me, the fact that the women who performed were all mind-blowingly excellent. I'd seen occasional storytelling shows before but nothing had prepared me for tales this honest or raw; the topic of love and lust had somehow brought out the perfect amount of vulnerability and humor. And so this show that I'd imagined as a one-off chance to read my book aloud suddenly became a monthly gig, with ads promoting it, more press than I could have imagined, and lines around the block. For once, the fact that I can be nearly impossible to please worked to my advantage as I scoured every site, show, and podcast I could find to hunt down the best women I could find to tell tales about lust and love. And for that effort, every month I've been able to see and hear the most amazing, inspiring women I've ever come across bare their hearts and souls by sharing tales of being rejected, disregarded, objectified, forgotten, and even, at times, abused. (It's not always that intense, of course; sometimes they're just talking about getting laid.)

Really, I came to see, the specific topic mattered a lot less than the fact that these women were making themselves the hero (or heroine, if you will) of every humiliation, heartbreak, or hellish date they'd experienced. The fact that they were all coming together and telling the truth about a part of life they'd long been taught to keep to themselves or at least only share with close friends has been undeniably therapeutic for me. And the fact that we've been lucky enough to attract incredibly warm and supportive audiences who laugh and groan and sometimes yell with identification as the performers elevate these experiences to incredibly humorous or deeply meaningful places (often both) leads me to believe that I'm not the only one feeling therapized. Though I never intended to create some sort of group counseling experience, the number of emails and postshow comments I've gotten from people telling me that what they've seen and heard has made them feel less alone proves, I guess, that you never know what can happen when you gather a group of women together.

But by the time I'd realized that, I'd had another realization, and this one came with a healthy dose of anxiety: because these women were taking the things that had happened to them and reframing them with the benefit of perspective, and doing it so well, I didn't want to suck in comparison to them. I'd also run out of passages from my memoir to read aloud after the first two shows. And so I had to learn to do this, too: to take experiences that had once left me in such despair that I couldn't uncurl my body from the fetal position—or had at least made me feel rejected, embarrassed, or ashamed—think about what I'd learned, and attempt to make that entertaining. It was one thing to do this in writing, but to do it on stage, where I'd have to see and hear, firsthand, if other people were relating or not, was genuinely terrifying. Honestly, some nights I think I said the word "like" from the stage more than I uttered the actual words of my story. And yet, through this act I've felt years of anger, sadness, and all sorts of other emotions I hadn't even realized I'd been clinging to crumble into the ether. Nothing I'd ever done before had the power to get me over something—or, in a few cases, some*one*—quite like standing on a stage telling the Lust & Love audiences about it. And so now, with this book, to be able to share all of this with an audience that can't necessarily make it to our L.A. show is thrilling in a way I can't quite articulate.

In order to organize the essays, I've divided them into three sections: Casual Sex, Dating, and Love—or Something Like It. These are not your run-of-the-mill sex, dating, and love stories. Casual sex rarely involves knocking into old ladies while making out with a gorgeous, Kierkegaard-reading Italian, as Laura Krafft describes in "À la Italia," or being frustrated by the tenderness of your Craigslist Casual Encounters hookup, as Claire Titelman so wittily describes in "Casual Friday." And while dating outside one's comfort level can certainly be a theme of dating stories, I don't believe romance with married men, younger men, older men, or men who believe they're Jesus has ever been as well described as it has been here by Cindy Chupack, Sara Benincasa, Anna Davies, and Diana Spechler, respectively. As for the Love—or Something Like It stories: well, prepare for Emma Straub to detail what it's like when your teen idol grows up; for Jillian Lauren to tell you what can happen when your inappropriate camp crush reciprocates; for Laura House to school you on what it's like to be a straight, liberated woman with her very own stripper; and for Meghan Daum to show how television can bond you to your spouse. And that's only the beginning.

That these women shared these tales with me and the True Tales audience fills me with pride. That I get to now pass them along to you only adds to the experience. That I get to do that without pressuring any of you to come to a reading is, I think, a boon for us all.

Anna David
September 2013

Casual Sex

À la Italia

Laura Krafft

*A*while ago, I was living in New York and about to celebrate a big birthday. An enormous birthday. The most colossal birthday I'd celebrated up to that point. I'm not going to say which it was but suffice it to say it was the first one where the number started becoming much smaller on the coasts than it was back home in the Midwest.

I decided to celebrate by taking myself to Italy. I'd always wanted to go and had never been. What better time than a birthday to become a citizen of the world? What better way to start than by being a tourist in Rome? In the summertime? At the height of tourist season? I tried to find a friend to travel with, but for some reason my plan didn't appeal to anyone. Most of my friends had traveled after college. A few said they would come but only if we went to small coastal, village-y, nontourist places. But I didn't want that. I wanted to see the sights. I decided to go it alone. I could do artisanal back in Brooklyn.

So I bought all the Rough Guides and pored over them. I planned every minute down to the second. I booked tours and lovely hotels, I made reservations at the best restaurants. And I got to Italy and I started touring around Rome and it was awful. Terrible in every way. I was so lonely. I hadn't thought about the fact that I had come from New York, where I sat alone at a desk all day before going back to an empty apartment, to Rome, where I would tour the sights alone all day before going back to an empty hotel room. Rome was basically New York with better footwear.

Also, nobody else in Italy was alone. Nobody. Everyone traveled around in clumps. I discovered that Italy is about friends and families and romance. Italy is not about being newly middle-aged and single. People had warned me that blondes in Italy have to put up with a lot of grabbing and whistling. This blonde, um, did not. Instead, there was a lot of solicitous moving out of my way and seating me at a table for one, away from the noise of joyful couples and families, in the back of the restaurant, next to the bathroom. I smelled so much human waste in Italy while trying to eat delicious food that, to this day, I have a hard time eating spaghetti. I remember covering my nose with a napkin while I ate and feeling like some kind of stately old widow in a Merchant Ivory film. The fact that I insisted on wearing European-y draped scarves around my neck and an expensive black fedora I'd bought on my first day made the humiliation complete.

But throughout it all, I tried to stay upbeat. I kept saying to myself, "I'm having a blast!" And I would pull out the beautiful leather journal I had bought specifically for the trip and write, "I am so lonely! I am so lonely!" over and over again. And I would carry the big, fancy camera I had bought specifically for the trip everywhere I went. And because I don't like to read camera manuals, I only took one picture. And the picture was blurry. And because the lens cap wasn't all the way off, the picture was also half dark. But I was in Italy and I kept reminding myself that even if it felt like I was fulfilling some weird karmic punishment, I was on the trip of a lifetime.

One day, in this spirit, I went on a tour of the Vatican Museum. I had booked a personal tour guide before I'd left New York, and, I will admit, I fantasized about how cool it would be if we fell in love. We did not. But I enjoyed the art. So much so that when the tour finished I thought, "Again!" And I went out to the enormous line and found another tour guide to give me a second tour because you can do that when you're traveling alone on the trip of a lifetime. Then I went to Trastevere, which the guidebooks had told me was the East Village of Rome, for the reservations I'd booked weeks earlier at a restaurant that was supposed to serve the best meatballs in Italy. And the meatball restaurant was closed. No explanation, just a locked door. But that was fine. I remember thinking it would make a great memory of the time I walked all the way to Trastevere because I was scared of cabs even though my legs were killing me because I'd been standing for ten hours. And how much fun it had been.

I went to the café across the street to have some wine and recalibrate. I wrote a couple "I'm so lonely" paragraphs in my journal and got a little buzzed. Then I looked around. There was a ridiculously beautiful guy sitting across from me, smoking a cigarette and reading Kierkegaard. He looked like he'd been sent over from central casting for the role of handsome intellectual type who doesn't realize that no one actually reads Kierkegaard and therefore doesn't know that you can lie and say you've read him and never be called on it— that Kierkegaard is in the same foolproof lie category as playing the harp or arc welding. I smirked at him and he looked at me and asked in Italian if I was laughing at him. I understood the gist of it and answered in English, "You're reading Kierkegaard in a café. It's a bit much, no?" Instead of being annoyed, he got all excited and said, "Ah, you speak English! If I buy you a drink, will you speak with me?" After a week of communicating by pointing and saying "Please" or "Thank you," I said "Yes" so fast I almost shrieked.

He came over to my table. His name was Allesandro and we talked for a while, the conversation drifting like so many conversations between New Yorkers and foreigners do onto the topic of whether or not the real New York City is anything like the New York City on the TV show *Friends*. Then he asked me cautiously, "Lah-oo-rah [that's me], would it be too much? This man, he is having a party. Would you come with me? He is the Warhol of Trastevere!" I obviously would. And I remember thinking it was funny that sometimes when God closes a meatball restaurant, he opens a Warhol party.

So we went to the party and the host did sort of look like Andy Warhol—if you caught him at the right angle. But better than that was the fact that it was a real Italian party in a real Roman apartment. Everyone was smoking. Everyone was laughing. The party passed in flashes of black-turtlenecked people explaining things to me with big hand gestures. I didn't understand a thing except that my new friend Allesandro kept filling my glass with wine.

When it ended, Allesandro and I went outside and he suddenly grabbed my hand and turned to me with a pained look in his eyes. "Lah-oo-rah," he said. "Can I ask you something? My heart, it is aching." I nodded and he asked, "Can I kiss you?" He looked at me beseechingly and I remember thinking, "Really? Who says that?" I mean, I was visiting from New York where guys never kissed me. The guys I went on dates with spent most of the night trying to clarify what would happen to our relationship if we took various next steps. I'd written the whole thing off as a world-wide phenomenon I called "Magic Dick Syndrome"—a syndrome wherein men think their penis is magic and that if you get even one whiff of it, you will become enchanted and want to marry them on the spot. Nobody I went on dates with in New York said, "My heart is aching." I don't know much but I know enough that when a handsome someone says that, you say, "Hell yes, I'll make out with you!" So we did. We made out all over Trastevere. We banged into old ladies carrying bread, stumble-walk kissed over bridges. We made out in the way only people in coffee commercials or catalogues do. It was fantastic.

After a while, Allesandro stepped back and asked very formally, "Lah-oo-rah, would you ever consider coming back to my apartment?" Before he could get the words out, I was like, "Hell yes, I'll go back to your apartment!" The next thing I knew, I was wearing a helmet and we were on his Vespa. His Vespa! We drove and drove, around fountains, on highways. The air rushing by smelled foreign and exotic. We ended up in a far-off suburb of Rome, at a weird postwar apartment building with huge front doors that had sixties-style doorknobs in the middle. It felt very Antonioni.

We went inside his apartment and made out all over the place. We had crazy, great sex. And I remember thinking to myself, "I'm alive! And I'm with this beautiful man! And this is really happening! Happy birthday to me! Happy birthday to me!" Afterward he cuddled with me in a way that only speakers of Romance languages can and I thought to myself, "I'm going to be okay with this part of my life." And we fell asleep.

The next morning, Allesandro and I woke up at the same time. And I looked at Allesandro and he looked at me and we both quickly drew back from each other and grunted the universal exclamatory, "Huh."

Then Allesandro said, "Lah-oo-rah, can I ask you something?" And I said, Of course. And he asked, "How *old* are you?" I looked at him and said haltingly, "Um . . . thirty . . ." And then I took a big pause while I tried to think of an age that wouldn't freak him out, and finished, ". . . -three?" I remember thinking, "I'm in Italy, I can dip low." And then I asked Allesandro how old he was and he answered haltingly, "Twenty . . ." and then there was an equally big pause while he thought of an age that wouldn't freak me out and finished, ". . . -five?"

And I realized that Allesandro was actually probably, like, twenty-one. And not just twenty-one but, like, secondary-sexual-characteristics-just-coming-into-play twenty-one. A new-hint-of-peach-fuzz twenty-one. And I realized, looking at his body, that what I had seen as reminiscent of a character from a Rossellini film was actually someone who was slender because he was still a boy. On the verge of manhood, getting close, but still, a boy.

Then I looked around his room and realized that what I had seen as great cuddling was actually clinging because we were on his tiny, single bed. And I saw stacks of books and realized he was reading Kierkegaard not because he was a philosopher-poet type, but because he was still in school and probably had a paper due on existential philosophers. And just as all this was clicking in, Allesandro asked if I would like him to make me an espresso and I said sure. He got up and started getting dressed. Then he stopped for a moment and solemnly asked me to promise that if I ran across his roommate, I would say that the coffee was mine because she always got mad when he used hers even though she used his toilet paper and he never said anything.

It was at that point that I remembered I had a reserved appointment at the Borghese Gallery. You have to get your entrance time months in advance, they're unavailable at the door, so I told Allesandro I had to leave.

He answered, "Of course, of course." And then asked, "Before you go, maybe we should . . ." He searched for the right way to phrase what was coming next and he was so sweet and polite because he was just a kid, and he asked, "Do you know what email is?" And it dawned on me that Allesandro was about to suggest we exchange email addresses but then had the thought I might be too old to know what that meant. I realized he thought of me the way I thought of my mother who, every time she goes to the ATM, needs to pull a little notebook out of her purse and look up her personal identification number—otherwise known as her PIN. Allesandro thought that as my mother was to the PIN, I was to email. To reiterate: he did not think I knew what email was.

I took a pen out of the little plastic pen cup on his desk and started writing all my information down. I told him that not only did I have an email address but I also had a Facebook page and had thoughts about starting a Tumblr. And then he showed me pictures from the soccer game he'd won the day before. And then I told him I had to leave.

It took several buses to get back to downtown Rome. They were all packed with the morning rush hour. Each time I got on, I would hold people up while I figured out the different fares. I didn't know where to stand because after touring the Vatican twice and then partying and having sex all night, I smelled foul. I didn't want to give my armpit too much access to fellow passengers' civil liberties. Nice old ladies kept giving me the stinkeye and then I would fall on them when the bus jostled.

When I finally got back to Rome, I took my stupid black hat out of my purse and put it on. I halfheartedly tied a scarf around my neck. It was at least 100 degrees. I wanted to take a cold bath back at my hotel but realized that I wouldn't have time to go there and make my entrance time at the Borghese Gallery. So I decided, "Screw it, I'm in Italy. Who will know?" And I trudged through the Villa Borghese gardens to the gallery.

Once there, I got in line behind a large touring group of ten-year-old soccer players from St. Louis and their mothers. Apparently, there had been a big international tournament that week. Everyone was freckle-faced. Everyone was adorable. I was older than all the mothers. As I was standing there, one of the kids turned to me and asked if I was an American. I'm not sure why he asked; the hat probably. "Yes," I told him. "I'm American." He told me he was from St. Louis and I told him I was from Illinois. He announced, "We just won our game." So I announced, "I just got laid."

My Sex Playlist

Alison Agosti

My longest relationship was my very first. We dated from when I was sixteen until I was twenty-one and he was my first love, my first kiss, my first person I ever slept with, and eventually my first heartbreak. Knowing myself better now than I did then, I understand why this fairly doomed relationship was able to survive that long. And even though it was a mostly mutual and inevitable breakup that we'd both been aware was coming for years, I was completely crushed, emotionally devastated in a way that only twenty-one-year-olds can be emotionally devastated. Now, at twenty-seven, I just can't muster up the kind of energy required to be able to stay up all night and get really upset about things. Who can be bothered? In fact, when I try to remember the last thing I was notably upset about, all I can come up with is an image of me walking past a display of leashes for cats and shaking my head.

I think part of the can't-get-out-of-bed sadness was due to the fact that I suddenly realized that romantic love was not unconditional and that I might have just experienced the last time I would be able to wholly give myself to another person without fear of getting hurt—hurt in a way where you ache with no cure.

A turning point in my devastation was about six months after we'd broken up, when I was finally able to go to the bathroom without crying. The reason this seemed significant was that the bathroom was the one place where I found it damn near impossible to fight off my thoughts, because it was the one place where I was always guaranteed to be alone. So I just remember it being a major landmark when I could finally sit there without tears.

The amazing thing is that I got over it. People would hug me and tell me that I was going to be okay and that time would heal my pain and whatever but when I was in the thick of it, there was no comfort and no consolation. My sadness had such a hold on me that I sobbed uncontrollably in the grocery store, in class, and while masturbating. And then it went away, and I was just left there with myself as I tried to learn how to be a person again.

And with depression's abrupt exit came the realization that I would eventually date someone else, which
would eventually lead to me sleeping with someone
else—someone else who I hadn't passed notes to in AP
English and whose high school swim meets I had never
attended and who I didn't know so completely that I
couldn't fall asleep without them. The idea of this was
so completely crazy to me that I realized that part of
the reason my ex and I had stayed together so long was
to avoid this very thing.

During college I worked at a hardware store, and I
remember talking to a coworker down aisle Q, which
was the farthest place from our boss and customers but
also the most likely place to see a rat, and telling her
about my dilemma. "I just can't imagine sleeping with
someone I'm not in love with," I said.

Thinking back on that, there's part of me that wants
to tell that girl she'd eventually sleep with people she
didn't even *like*, over and over again. Dating, even
now, feels very much like a competition between two
people—like a race to figure the other one out without
revealing too much before the other person does. It
should go without saying that I am terrible at dating.

The way I decided to trick myself into excitement
was to make an extensive and painfully planned-out sex
playlist, even though I understood that sex in college was
sort of like a tiny bird trapped in a house just frantically

trying to get back outside, unsure of where an open window was. The optimism of young women can be heartbreaking. Please keep in mind that, at this point in the story, dating was completely hypothetical; there wasn't a long line to take out the girl who had been spontaneously sobbing for most of junior year. But I knew at some point in my life I was going to be in the position to have sex again, even if it wasn't for another ten years, so let's just say that it was a sort of very optimistic sex playlist. When it was finished, it was about three hours long and broke down into roughly four parts:

PART ONE: A few innocuous pop songs so I could bail if it turned out I was misreading the situation;

PART TWO: Make-out slow jams, with Feist's album *Let It Die* prominently featured;

PART THREE: Songs with a harder bass for the actual fucking part (thank God for the Black Keys);

PART FOUR: The denouement. Where, in my mind, we would talk about our feelings while Sigur Rós serenaded us.

Making a perfect playlist is not unlike a game of Jenga: there has to be balance and precision, and sometimes adding one thing will make it awkward or top-heavy. So there were revisions and there was thoughtful planning and there were many discussions with friends—all things I preferred to do rather than focus my energy and free time on going out and meeting someone. I may be bad at dating but I do make an excellent mix.

This was in 2005, which was a great music year. Spoon's *Gimme Fiction*, My Morning Jacket's *Z*, and LCD Soundsystem's two-disc self-titled album *that changed my soul* all came out and thus all made appearances on the sex playlist. The year 2005 felt like it was very much invested in getting me laid. I looked over that playlist recently, and it totally holds up. Maybe sprinkle in some Frank Ocean and a pinch of Miguel and I could make it work for me today.

Still, it was a year before I got the opportunity to use that thing. There was a long, long, *long* dry spell where I just had sweaty palms and weird sex dreams about Benjamin McKenzie from *The O.C.* while sleep-humping my pillow. Then, finally, I met a guy in one of my many women's lit classes named Jonathan. "Not John," he would correct you if you called him John and really, that tells you everything you need to know about him. Jonathan looked and dressed like a rugged J.Crew model, but he was actually very frail and small. I felt like he could just blow away at any moment and something about that was very attractive to me. So one day I somehow tricked this tiny, delicate man into coming back to my apartment.

Being in a relationship during those important years where you are discovering what courtship is and how to express and receive romantic affection had really fucked me up, man. I mean, the fact that I thought I needed to *trick* a twenty-one-year-old into coming back to my place to have sex is absurd, when I could have just politely *asked*. I told you, I'm bad at this whole thing.

Not long after Jonathan and I were sitting down on my small and uncomfortable IKEA couch, we started making out. This was my chance. Sex—and my sex playlist—was going to happen. I went over to my laptop and pushed play on my masterpiece. Or I thought I did.

Instead, "Stand by Me" started to play. If you're not familiar with the song (which come on, yes you are) it's the one that begins, "When the night has come and the land is dark / And the moon is the only light we'll see." According to Wikipedia, there are over four hundred recorded versions of the song in existence and I had at least twelve of them on my computer, saved under a playlist titled "Our Song" because that was the song that the five-year ex and I had danced to at junior prom, I think? Isn't that how you end up with a designated song that you will ultimately end up hating or crying to or both? Also, can we please ignore the fact that I still had it on my computer a year and a half after we'd broken up?

As soon as the song started playing, I knew what had happened. I knew I'd clicked on the wrong thing, and I knew what was about to unfold: twelve versions of a very short and recognizable song were about to play and there was no way that this was going to go unnoticed by Jonathan, who was so beautiful and delicate and sensitive. But instead of just turning back around to the computer and correcting my mistake, which would have taken three seconds tops, I decided to let it ride.

I walked back to the couch as Ben E. King's soulful original started playing, and immediately realized that it was way too sexual. It's also a song that is meant for something important, and Jonathan-not-John was never going to be important. We started making out in spite of this and at first all was fine. I figured I was finally going to be able to see what was happening underneath all of that gingham. Then, at about version three, Jonathan pulled away.

"Is this 'Stand by Me?'" he asked. There was a hint of confusion in his voice but he certainly wasn't upset yet. And so I calmly replied that yes, it was (I believe we were on the Otis Redding cover, which is great, by the way).

"But," he said, now sounding slightly annoyed, "is this like the third time 'Stand by Me' has played?" This would have been my second opportunity to correct the situation. I could have easily said, "Oh, weird. Let me change it." But I didn't do that. Because that would have been normal and at that moment I was quite terrified of everything—terrified that I was about to have sex with this guy, terrified that I might cry afterward, terrified that he would think my boobs looked weird or that I would be rusty and terrible at the whole thing. So instead of doing the normal thing, I shook my head, gave him a brow furrow, and said, "No." Just that, "No."

And he let it go. Which felt like a true miracle.

We got back into it. Clothes were coming off! He was as pale as I had hoped and it seemed like sex was about to happen. Then the Ike and Tina Turner version came on and he pulled away again.

"Okay, this is definitely 'Stand by Me.'" To which I agreed that yes, it was. His response, now clearly more than a little bit annoyed, was, "But it's like the sixth version of 'Stand by Me' that we've heard." I was now deep in this thing so it felt like the only thing I could do was just give him a half-naked shrug as though we should just agree to disagree on how many versions of "Stand by Me" we'd heard. After all, it could have been the seventh or eighth version.

I tried to lean back in but Jonathan-not-John pushed me off and stood up. He looked down at me, both of us nearly naked, and, with a finger pointed at me, he said, "You are a liar." And then he said nothing else as he collected his clothes and exited my apartment with "Stand by Me" continuing to play maniacally in the background. And I just listened to the versions by Jimi Hendrix, Seal, and Alvin and the Chipmunks as I lay in stunned silence for the next few minutes.

The thing with storming out of someone's apartment in college is that you will inevitably run into each other again. With Jonathan, that moment came the following Monday morning, when I walked into the lecture hall where I'd first laid eyes on his waif nerd body. Out of sheer embarrassment, I didn't say a word to him through the following three more classes and final we had. I'm not sure if it was awkwardness, Jonathan-not-John-ness, or the belief that I was insane that kept him from talking to me.

To this day, I still have not gotten to use that sex playlist.

Jammin' Java Joe

Sacha Z. Scoblic

Justin was actually much better looking than Jimmy Fallon, who was at the time my favorite *Saturday Night Live* player. And yet, as the vodka sloshed behind my eyes, I kept seeing Jimmy Fallon every time Justin turned toward me. Some of these times, I would rub my eyes, shake my head, loosen up, roll my shoulders, and then look straight at Justin. And, for a moment, there he would be: officially very cute, no need to super-impose Jimmy Fallon over him. But within seconds, it would happen again; the veil would descend and I would find myself talking to Jimmy. Looking back on it now, I think my subconscious was trying to tell me something about Justin's charms, not his appearance. I wasn't beer-goggling his looks; I was beer-goggling his personality.

Back in my twenties, my close friend Ivy had orga-
nized a girls' weekend to Las Vegas. Ivy grew up in
the kind of close-knit Chicago family who makes a
trip to Vegas several times a year—the way my family
might go antiquing. So this weekend jaunt was par for
the course for Ivy—a tough gambler, school principal,
and engrossing conversationalist, who often knocks
me out with a single question. "Do you think mutual
respect or shared values is more important in a relationship?" she once asked me in her casual and yet
deeply interested way. Back then, I would marvel at
her fascination with moral questions and reach for
the wispy threads of integrity dangling out of reach
in my mind. Words like "values" and "respect" were
not yet even on my list of relationship musts, which at
that point really only included "intimidatingly smart"
and "hysterically funny." I liked in particular to scoff
at men who thought books were objects one could
leave behind once one left college and at those who
thought Dane Cook was awesome. Which brings us
to Justin.

Our friend Emily came with Ivy and me to Vegas
and promptly asked her old camp pal, Justin, to come
and hang out. Justin was a native of Las Vegas and the
marketing director for an SAT test-prep company in
the area. It all sounded so normal.

"I didn't think people actually lived in Vegas," I said

to Ivy and Emily. "You know, except for showgirls and magicians."

"It's like the fastest growing city in America, Sach," said Ivy.

"I guess I never really believed that," I said, as though such statistics were matters of opinion, and I suddenly became unnerved by the kind of person who thinks it's normal to raise children in Las Vegas and send them to, say, SAT test-prep courses in the shadow of a city in which strip clubs, casinos, and Celine Dion pass for culture.

But Justin seemed perfectly well adjusted and exceptionally good looking. And, after dinner with the girls—and after several cocktails and bottles of wine—we met Justin at a bar and he even seemed "hysterically funny." He had, of course, also morphed into Jimmy Fallon at that point. And though I never found him "intimidatingly smart," a night on the town with Jimmy, er, Justin, seemed like a very Las Vegas thing to do.

I remember a nightclub, the kind of cheesy place where the guys wear too much gel in their hair and the girls look a lot more like MTV spring breakers than, well, I do or ever did. It was like disco dancing at a reality show casting call. There were a lot more laser-light-show effects, Usher remixes, fake boobs, and faker tans than I was comfortable with. I feared it was only a matter of time before I ended up in a hot tub while also being on television. So, I remember saying, "Hell yes, Jimmy Fallon," when Justin asked me if I wanted to get out of there. I also remember saying goodbye to my girlfriends. I was on the heels of a breakup and I thought that spending the night with someone who wouldn't ask me about that would be a lot better than hanging out with the good friends who would.

In the next scene—for my memory has elided segments of the evening and edited the night into a short film—Justin and I were at an Irish pub. Or at least what passes for such in Vegas. It was a brand-new-but-made-to-look-old pub with brass rails along the bar and four-leaf clovers dotting the wood-paneled walls.

"I thought this might be more your scene," Justin said as he carried two of the largest steins of beer I have ever encountered.

I'm not sure what about me screamed, "Fake authentic Irish pub, please," but, when the actually-from-Ireland Irish band started up nice and loud, complete with total audience participation, I didn't have to worry about keeping up a conversation. This was never more of a relief than when, during the band's break, Justin said, "That's what I love about Vegas. You don't have to travel because every place you'd want to go is already right here."

"Shhhh, Jimmy Fallon," I said, hand reaching up

to silence him. *Drink more, Sacha. Drink more.* And I dove back into my novelty-sized beer stein. Though, when the band covered the Violent Femmes in full Irish brogue, I was legitimately delighted with the choice of bar and began belting out "Blister in the Sun" with the regulars. (Or were they just handpicked codgers meant to look like genuine regulars in an Irish bar so that people like me would feel like I was having an authentic experience? *Vegas is meta,* I thought.)

But then we were in a new scene. We were now at a bar in the middle of one of those Las Vegas hallway malls—you know, in case you felt like puking in the Gucci store. The bar was in the shape of a large white orb—like being inside a bubble or maybe a geodesic dome. The drinks were all brightly colored: red, purple, and blue martinis bobbed along against the white bubble walls. *Want more, want more.*

"It's like being in space, right?" Justin asked, eyes wide and smiling, thrilled to be introducing me to Judy Jetson's favorite bar.

"You're funny, Jimmy Fallon."

"Why do you keep calling me that?"

"Shhhh."

Scene change: sunlight is streaming through the curtains across a very lived-in bedroom. Laundry is heaped here and there, a model airplane rests on a desk, there are small trophies on a bookshelf, and a poster of a

Lamborghini tacked to the wall. This is not my hotel room. *How the fuck did I get into a ten-year-old boy's room?* Suddenly, I am all too aware that the sunlight is new, that it is early, like 7-AM-and-I-went-to-bed-at-4-AM early. But I have the energy of the displaced, the vigor of the shamed. I simply want nothing more than to teleport back to my own hotel bed and wake up in the afternoon as though this never happened.

"Good morning," says a chipper voice in the doorway. Justin. *Okay, no big deal. Justin is Emily's friend. He's a nice, hot guy. Not the worst outcome.* Justin leans in the doorway, shirtless but wearing cargo shorts and sneakers as though he has just spent the last hour mowing the lawn. *No, not the worst outcome.*

"Hi," I rasp, sounding a lot more like Stevie Nicks than I had anticipated. "Where are we?"

"My house!"

"Your house?"

"Well, my parents' house. But don't worry, they're on vacation."

And, until that moment, I had not been worried at all that his parents might actually be here or on vacation or in any way proximate—because why on earth would they be? I mean, unless you took a girl to your parents' house instead of to your own house. But why would you take a girl to your parents' house? When it occurs to me—

"Um, Justin, do you live with your parents?"

"I'm saving a lot of money, dude."

A peek out the window confirms that I am in the midst of a labyrinth of suburban tract homes. There is nary a tree—or any piece of the natural world, for that matter—in sight, and endless replicas of the same sandy-hued house and two-car garage unfold into the distance over and over again. Waves of suburban sameness wash over me, pushing me back, marooning me farther and farther away from the anonymity of my cheesy Vegas hotel room. Ivy was right about Vegas's fast growth; this sea of expansion looks like it fell off the back of a flatbed truck preassembled in the middle of the night.

"Why are you up so early?" I ask in another barfly rasp that makes me sound like a sixty-something old maid who smokes unfiltered cigarettes, puts her lipstick on by feel, and kisses her pugs on the mouth—all of which serves to make me feel more and more out of place in the arrested development of Justin's childhood (and, apparently, adulthood) bedroom.

"I promised my parents I'd clean the pool before they came back," says Justin.

I decide not to question why he felt the crack of dawn was the right time to do this chore. But if it's an invitation to go swimming, I'm passing. I am just grateful he is alert and can take me back to the city, to a room that does not make me feel like a child molester. At this point a room that makes me feel just plain slutty would be great.

This is when Justin turns his back to me to open the door to his closet. And there, in the fresh sunlight and splashed across the entirety of his back, is the most insane and mortifying thing I have ever seen. It is a tattoo. But it is not a massive dragon or a red heart that says mom or a Chinese character or any of the thousands of inane but entirely expected tattoos one might imagine. The tattoo is a cartoon man, a kind of stick figure Rastafarian (there are definitely dreadlocks emerging from its circle head) who is half dancing and half drinking a cup of coffee, arms akimbo, a mug in one hand. It is a happy Jamaican coffee drinker. It is a cartoon, but it also has the simplicity of a logo. The phrase "Jammin' Java Joe" ricochets in my head for a second, but then disappears. And I just gape at what has to be the least badass, most ridiculous, and possibly even racist tattoo that has ever seen the light of day. What self-respecting tattoo artist would even agree to render this embarrassment on a man's back—let alone on the *entirety* of a man's back?

"Awesome, right?" asks Justin when he looks over his shoulder and notices that my jaw has unhinged itself from my body and landed on the floor. And I am embarrassed—not for me, but for Justin. *No, sweet, simple*

Justin. Nooo. Bad idea. Baaad. And then, as if saving the worst for last, Justin finds the T-shirt he's apparently been rooting around in the closet for. He pulls it over his head; the T-shirt is threadbare light yellow, and in small letters across the chest, it reads: JAMMIN' JAVA JOE, MON. KINGSTON, JAMAICA. And I am already thinking, *No, no, no,* as he turns around to reveal a very colorful and large image of, well, Jammin' Java Joe on the back of the shirt. And as the fabric slides down Justin's back, the cartoon on the T-shirt neatly falls into place in perfect scale over the tattoo on Justin's body. Like lining up a tracing-paper illustration. An exact copy. Just like all the houses on his block.

Back at the hotel, Ivy and Emily scream with laughter when I tell them about Jimmy Fallon, when I tell them about the Lamborghini poster, and when I finally tell them about the Jammin' Java Joe full-back tattoo. "I think I've even seen that T-shirt before," I say. "I think it's like a popular tourist shirt in Jamaica." And that is when Emily confesses that Justin has been wearing that T-shirt since she met him at camp; that scrap of cloth must be at least fifteen years old. "He must be totally obsessed with it," she says. And we all fall across each other in tears, laughing.

"I wish you had stayed around last night," Ivy says to me later. And I wish that as well. Why would I ditch a group of girls I have known since college and rarely see—none of whom live in the same city as I do—for Jammin' Java Joe? I realize the answer is easy: intimacy was precisely what I wanted to avoid that night. I didn't leave my best friends for some guy; I left my best friends for more mindless drinking—a lot more than I would have gotten away with if I'd stayed with them. I wanted more alcohol, more fun, more Vegas, more Jimmy Fallon, more alcohol, more, more, more. So I took it.

And that is when I realize: I did not do Vegas with Jimmy Fallon last night. Nope. I fucked Jammin' Java Joe.

Deep-Fried Southern Sex

Amy Dresner

*H*e was ugly but sexy ugly with blinding charisma and searing wit. He had a reputation as a ladies' man, which should have put me off but just made him more alluring. You know how we women delude ourselves into thinking that we will be the one that will tame him? *He has never met a woman as special as me,* we think.

He spoke with a growl, a low-pitched Southern drawl that was a remnant of his youth in South Carolina. I guess he would have been considered a redneck but to me, as a Beverly Hills Jew, that seemed exotic and exciting—like some wild animal that you don't see in the zoos of Los Angeles. He always wore a trucker cap and a funny T-shirt. I remember one he sported regularly that said KILL 'EM ALL AND LET GOD SORT 'EM OUT. For our purposes, we will call him Carl.

I remember the first time I met him. It was in the rooms where lushes and junkies congregate to try to kick their habits. This particular meeting was in the lower bar of a big cheesy metal club. Hipsters would talk about the joy of sobriety while staring at rows of pretty bottles behind a low bar. He had a gray buzz cut and ice-blue eyes. I was coming off of shooting coke and I was skinny and shaking, wearing a parka in the summer, shivering from the snow that still coursed through my veins.

A stunning brunette with hot pants and high-heeled fringe boots introduced me to him as her ex-boyfriend. *She fucked him*, I thought incredulously. It lit a curiosity in me.

"Ohhh, look at me, I used to shoot coke, I weigh six pounds," he said when we met as he danced around like a marionette.

After the meeting, I asked the beauty, "Did you really used to date that weathered old man?" She nodded and said in a matter-of-fact way, "Yes, I like white guys that look like they just got out of prison." That framed him in a whole new light.

A few weeks later, at another meeting, he gave me his seat. If nothing else, Southerners are gentlemen. I was charmed. At the break, he walked over and tickled my arm.

"Ooh that feels nice," I purred.

"I know what I'm doing," he said.

Afterward, we were all having lunch at the Silver Spoon, this dive on Santa Monica Boulevard that Shelley Winters was known to drink at. There was a tableful of us, all ex-drunks, bonding and chatting— "fellowshipping" as it's known in the program. Carl talked about some girl who'd been trying to have sex with him the night before.

"She texted me, 'I'm going to get my period tomorrow so tonight is our last chance,'" he told us. "I told her, 'I'll fuck you on your period—I'd fuck if you had diarrhea.'" And with that, he skewered a piece of sausage on his fork and chewed it defiantly.

Something inside me jumped. His primal take-no-prisoners sex drive lit something in me that I'd never felt before. I had to have him.

When I got home, my power was out and I used it as an excuse to contact him. I shot him a text: "My power is out. Zero television or power for my wall-powered vibrator. What's a horny princess to do?"

"Well maybe some nice gentleman will let you come over and watch his television."

Then my power miraculously went back on. Damn.

"Just go use your vibrator and yell my name when you come. God told me to protect you from me."

"Ahhh, a player with altruistic as well as religious convictions. Nothing could be sexier."

"Come over," he wrote. "God said you're on your own."

As I was driving over, I asked if he wanted me to stop and bring him anything.

"Just you on your knees, gagging on my cock."

I felt scared, as if my bravado had just sold me a bill of goods I wasn't prepared to pay for. But there was no turning back now.

I arrived at his apartment, a tiny, smoke-filled one-bedroom set off from the street in Hollywood. The walls were covered with scary clown paintings and portraits of Jesus, his shelves brimming over with adult cartoons and cheesy horror movies. Yikes.

"Come lay down," he ordered. He was on the bed, fully clothed, watching TV. I took off my shoes and lay next to him. He quietly reached over and held my hand. My heart was pounding furiously in my chest. I suddenly turned over to face him and began to kiss him.

"Oh my, you're an aggressive little thing," he said.

Clothes quickly came off. His forearms were tattooed like a sailor's. He was older but fit. I was fatter than I'd been in a while and felt uncomfortably curvy.

"You've got such a hot body," he purred. "Nice tits."

My eyes were closed. I felt timid.

"Look in my eyes," he barked. "I wanna see you."

He opened my legs briefly and put his face to my pussy. Then he came back up and put my legs over his shoulders, like a wheelbarrow, the position for deepest thrusting.

"I don't come," I warned. "Like ever. I just wanted you to know." I felt stupid right after I said it.

"That's okay, I always come," he replied.

He began to fuck me. He had a big dick. I was so wet I was embarrassed, mad that my body was betraying me.

"Open your pussy," he said. "Let me in."

It felt as if he wanted all of me, even for just the moment. I felt shy. I said nothing.

Suddenly there was a flood of fluid.

"What was that?" I asked, concerned. Had I just gotten my period?

"That was you coming, unless you're pregnant and I just broke yer water."

He pulled out right before he came and ejaculated all over my tits. I saw him towering over me and he looked so beautiful and I thought, "Oh my God, I love him." I rubbed him all over me. I didn't want to waste a drop.

He padded off to the bathroom and when he came back, I said, "I'm hungry. Wanna go eat?"

"Are you really hungry or do you just wanna spend more time with me so you don't feel like a whore?"

"I don't feel like a whore—I've got no problem with fucking you and going home," I lied.

"Yeah, let's go eat, you Jew. I only eat at my favorite local diner so that better be okay with you."

I nodded politely, submissively.

As we walked into the diner, people at every booth greeted him. The entire waitstaff knew him intimately. He was, indeed, a regular. And I could tell by the look in their eyes that I was just the girl du jour, the special of the day.

I went off to the bathroom and when I returned, a girl I recognized from the rooms was chatting with Carl. As I approached, she shot me a dirty jealous look and walked away.

"Does she know I just fucked you?" I asked.

"Of course. Everybody fucking knows," he said nonchalantly.

When the bill came, I paid for dinner. Boy, did I pay.

The Accidental Groupie

Taylor Orci

*I*n my early twenties I got a journalism internship in DC. It was really great; I got to do a lot of things, and one of the things I got to do was interview this band. I'm not gonna say the name, but it's probably in your top ten indie bands of all time. Especially if you're a guy who likes button-down plaid shirts with pearl snaps and words like "eclectic." If you like that, this is your favorite alt-country band. I, however, didn't like their music. I thought it was slow and twangy.

I should say, though, that I didn't have much of a taste in music at this point. Not like I have an impeccable taste in music now, but at the time I had only started liking "cool" music about two years earlier. And by "cool" I mean anything that wasn't derivative of the Indigo Girls or Gene Krupa. If you don't know who Gene Krupa is, ask your grandparents.

But it didn't matter if I liked the music or not. I was excited to interview a real band!

The guys in the band were really nice. There was this one guy in particular who was being *really* nice, and after the interview he gave me a backstage pass to the show they were playing that night. And after the show, he cornered me and kissed me. No one had ever cornered me and kissed me before. And after Mr. Band kissed me—let's call him Jake—after Jake kissed me, he said, "I just wanna say I think you're really beautiful, and you should come to Cleveland with us tonight." I knew what could happen in Cleveland—I'd seen *Almost Famous*. Cleveland was where I could run down the hallway of some fancy hotel in my well-planned flirty underwear holding a bottle of real champagne, exclaiming, "It's all happening!" But I told him no, because I took my unpaid internship seriously. And because I realized I had a serious lack of cool underwear.

Eventually my internship ended and Jake and I stayed in touch. He wrote me postcards—he wrote me two postcards—but the postcards said things like, "I miss you," and "I'm in the birthplace of Brigitte Bardot, she's got nothing on you." And I'd think, "Oh my God, I'm dating someone famous!" I had never really *dated* anyone before and now I wasn't just dating a guy, I was dating a *man*! A Famous Man! Man, did I feel important.

But after a few casual emails, phone calls, and post-cards, everything stopped. Still, that wasn't any reason in my mind to think we weren't still dating. In fact, the less we talked, the more I filled in the blanks with my own imagination. I thought, *Maybe he's not texting me because he's too busy planting secret messages to me in his live shows*—I really thought this. So I'd find the band's live performances online and listen for any secret references (there weren't any, by the way). I downloaded the band's entire discography *and* Jake's solo projects to try to get a glimpse into this guy's brain. I joined nearly all the message boards for this band, and there were a lot of fans and a lot of message boards. And I had a copy of the tour schedule so after each show I'd go online and I'd go on these message boards and see if anybody said something mean about the performance—so I could be a defender of this man I was dating.

This took up *hours* of my day. And I'm pretty sure that the textbook definition of an obsession is when you do something so much it interferes with your everyday life, but that didn't occur to me. All I was thinking was, *I'm in love! Or . . . a famous guy compared me to Brigitte Bardot! Same thing! Who cares! Whatever!*

So for months I heard nothing. Then one day, I got a phone call out of the blue and it was Jake, and he said, "Hey"—really casual—"Hey, I'm gonna be playing

Coachella tomorrow. You should come down and be my date."

So, I drove six hours to go to Coachella. Casually, of course. And when I got to the festival, I called him and he was like, "I'm busy." So I wandered around alone for a few hours—I got one of those Drumstick ice cream cones and tried not to think about how I was basically at the beck and call of some guy I knew nothing about short of his page on Wikipedia. And in the process it started to dawn on me that *maybe* I was getting used. But then I saw a group of hot girls wearing the band's T-shirt and that made me forget about feeling used and remember how *special* I was. After all, he wasn't with them; he had chosen me.

Eventually he allowed me backstage to watch the band play—it felt like such a privilege to watch a band play from backstage in front of thousands of fans. Then I heard someone in back of me go, "Where did all these groupies come from?" And I thought, *What groupies? I don't see any groupies.* Me, who wasn't there for the music but for the eye contact of Jake as he was wailing away on his Moog. I fought off the idea that the groupies he was referring to could have included me. Instead, I just kept dancing to attract attention to myself, vying for more eye contact.

And after the show, even though during the drive over, I'd kept telling myself, "I'm not gonna sleep with this guy, I'm not gonna sleep with this guy," we slept together, mostly 'cause I thought with all the special treatment I was getting, to not have sex with him would have just been rude. But after we had sex—and I don't know if this was because he was drunk or what—he kind of curled up and just started crying, saying how lonely he was, how he had fought off depression. And then he went off on this long rant about his battles with suicide and about loneliness, and it seemed so weird to me how someone in this iconic band felt so alone. But instead I stroked his hair and said things like, "It's just because you're so creative!" And, "No one understands you!" 'Cause I understood him. Right?

Then we passed out, and in the morning the phone rang, and I picked it up, and the woman on the other line said, "Mrs. [the guy's last name], this is your wake-up call." And this was a wake-up call in more ways than one. Because the morning was very awkward, and the vulnerable guy I had seen the night before was gone. We went down to eat in the lobby, where we ate our Froot Loops in silence. I looked around me and the hotel restaurant was full of similar scenes going on: lots of older rocker-looking men with younger-looking girls picking at cold omelettes and stale muffins and not talking to each other—including the other members of the band, all of whom had wives and girlfriends back home. That's when it sank in that I had become an accidental groupie to a band I hadn't really liked in the first place.

And I get it now; they're a good band. And my bad experience with one of the guys doesn't negate their artistry or whatever. After Kobe Bryant was accused of statutory rape, Nutella didn't drop his endorsement, because he's awesome at basketball. When a person's abilities are exceptional, we see the artist apart from his humanity. We put aside their character flaws for the sake of society's cultural enrichment. Slow clap for us.

Looking back on it, I'd like to think that Jake wasn't just trying to use me for sex, that the postcards meant something; maybe he really did like me at first but over the course of knowing me, discovered I was too young and giggly—which I was. I mean, as I realized just how famous this guy's band was, I kind of lost my shit. Maybe that's why he felt so lonely, because chicks like me couldn't see past his fame.

So before you think alt-country rockers don't have groupies and instead sit around all day talking about their feelings while canning their own fruit preserves, you should really think again. Show business is show business, no matter how much shaggy hair and vintage flannel you try to throw on it.

Casual Friday

Claire Titelman

I met Avi, a depressed comedian, while working on a Subway commercial. We were both playing losers who work at a crappy sandwich shop competitor. If only we could be appealing enough to work at Subway! We bonded over that desire. And by "bonded" I mean we got naked in my trailer at lunch. Before it got really exciting he was like, "Just FYI, I'm in the market for something casual." And I was like, "Oh good thing because I'm wearing my cotton period underwear. That's casual, right?"

The truth is that I'm a serious person, sex included. I practically frown when I orgasm.

"Have you ever had casual sex?"

"No . . ."

"Then how do you know you don't like it? You can't not like something that you've never tried."

"Really?" I ask. "Because I don't like murder."

Casual sex is a lot like drugs. At first glance you're like *I would never try that it's bad and I'm a good girl* and then you're like *Okay you can spank me, guy-who-won't-call-the-next-day, but just this one time* and then suddenly it's *GIVE IT TO ME EVERY DAY I DON'T CARE IF I LOSE MY JOB AND ALL MY TEETH FALL OUT.*

Once I got a taste of sex where commitment and cuddling were replaced by freedom and spanking, I was hooked. It was very eye- and vagina-opening.

On a hot Friday night in August, an hour before we are supposed to meet, I get a call from Avi. "I'm sorry, Claire, I totally want to go to the planetarium and have oral sex under the stars but I'm getting side effects from this new antidepressant and I think I'm going to throw up." Realizing he can no longer make sweet non-love to me, I do what any girl would do who's horny and lonely and sitting on a lumpy twin bed in an un-air-conditioned room of her best friend GJ's parents' house in South Pasadena because she's had to sublet her lovely Venice apartment having found herself deeply in debt: I browse Craigslist Casual Encounters.

I'm not actually going to respond to any of them. I'm just going to read the lewd requests, pretend I'm a body without a soul, and masturbate. I browse the list in hopes of finding something sexy. There's the usual stuff: a JPEG of a big curvy penis just seemingly floating in midair, a bunch of pics of porn star threesomes obviously pulled from Google Images but with captions like "This was from my last bukkake," and even a familiar face, a guy who runs the camera at a casting office where I audition who wants to "unfold a woman onto the fur rug in front of his fireplace and lay into her like a drill looking for oil." Well, small world! It's moments like these you realize you really are part of a larger community with like-minded people.

And then I come upon a listing that says, "I'm an artist looking for my muse." What a coinkydink—I make collages so I'm an artist, too! And my grandma once wrote a lullaby inspired by me when I was a baby so I guess I'm also kind of a muse. He includes a photo of his face and not just his genitals, which is a nice gesture, and says he's up for anything, "gentle or hard." A Renaissance man—I like it! And suddenly I think, *What's the difference between casual sex with Avi who I barely know and casual sex with some other penis I barely know? I'm in.*

I can't email him from my Gmail account because I don't want him to know my last name, so I have to open up a new account (this Craigslist Casual Encounters thing sure is a lot of work). I need an alias, so I call myself Midnight Elm (my cat's name plus the street I grew up on—'cause that's how the porn stars do it). He writes back immediately, saying he wants a pic and that he won't meet without seeing what I look like. I respond, "Don't worry. You won't be disappointed." And it's not that I think I'm a Victoria's Secret model, it's just I think one's hopes for one's Craigslist Casual Encounter is not unlike one's hopes for one's unborn child: if it's got fingers, toes, and no AIDS, you're good to go!

We agree to meet at a bar in his neighborhood of Los Feliz. He asks, "But how will I know it's you? What will you be wearing?" I don't know . . . a tube top? A push-up bra? A bikini? A ball gown? Wait, this is a *casual* encounter, right? In that case, I'll be wearing what I wear every day. "A navy blue cardigan." You can take a girl outta Massachusetts but you're not gonna get her to take off her navy blue cardigan. "Oh, and I wear glasses." "Glasses?" he asks. "I love glasses." Cool, maybe he wants kinky schoolgirl sex. I'll bring the fake braces that were made for me on a Verizon commercial just in case.

෬

He looks like guys I'm friends with and have dated. Creative, professional. He asks me what I like to drink. I don't drink, so I don't know what to say, but I spot a poster with a Hawaiian lady dancing that says rum, so I say, "Rum."

"And Coke?"

I don't drink caffeine either. "No, just rum."

"Straight?"

"Yeah silly, I'm straight, why would I be here if I was into girls . . . are you a girl?"

"No, I meant the rum. Straight rum sounds kinda harsh."

"Oh, yeah, I'm not actually going to drink it!"

"You want me to get you a drink you aren't going to drink?"

"Yes, I want to hold it." For God's sake, I'm about to have anonymous and degrading sex with you so I want to hold this for a few minutes and I want you to buy it for me!

We walk back to his place on Hillhurst. It's a perfect little bungalow on a street I've always wanted to live on—cute shops and restaurants, near Griffith Park. He tells me he's going to New York for a few months and wants to sublet it but is worried about letting it to a stranger. Wait, will I stop being a stranger after we have sex? Because I could be the subletter, and when my friends say, "Oh, cute place, where'd you find it?," I'll be able to honestly say, "Craigslist."

He sits down and starts caressing my face and tells me how pretty I look. I want to say: *But I'm a slut.* He says, "You seem so nice." *A dirty nasty slut!* "Where did you go to college?" *University of Slutting.* "Where

do your parents live?" *Massachuseyourownslutts.* "Are
they married?" *I don't have parents and I'm from the
street, okay?!*

He tells me that he's newly divorced and has been
trying to date but striking out. "It's so hard to meet
good people in Los Angeles," he says. And then he asks
if he can hold my hand. "I can't explain it, but I just
really like you, you know?"

Now that I'm with him, it's obvious I've made a
big mistake. I want to scream, "I don't want an artist
looking for his muse!" I want a dom looking for his
sub, a lesbian who wants to give a nonlesbian her first
time, the "masseuse-in-training" who wants to give me
a free full-body rubdown and "just see where it goes,"
the guy who wants me to "lick his pinis and suck his
bulls" (I don't care that he can't spell, his "pinis"
looks huge). At this point, I'd even prefer the father-
grandfather team who've clearly been burned before,
judging by their stern disclaimer: "You must be into
both fathers *and grandfathers.*" What I actually say is,
"Same here! Just looking to have a nice evening, meet
a nice guy. You seem really great." God, I'm such a
people pleaser. I can't even tell my casual encounter
what I want in bed. My therapist is not going to be
proud of me come Monday morning.

As if he can hear my inner dialogue, he asks me, "So,
Claire, what do *you* want to do?"

What do *I* want to do? I'm getting a second chance!
I smile coyly and say, "Well, your listing did say you're
up for gentle or *hard* . . ."

"Yeah, I'm up for anything."

Great!

"As long as it's not weird, of course. Did you want
to do something weird?"

Weird? I'm not weird. Do I look weird? No, I was
just trolling around Casual Encounters because I want
to lie down and have you bed me like we're an unhap-
pily married couple. Yes, I want WEIRD! Maybe at
some point I'm going to actually grow up and, who
knows, have a family, so if I'm ever going to get weird,
now's the time.

Dude.

Let's.

Weird.

Out.

Instead I lie down and stare at the ceiling while he
whispers, "You're so pretty," and kisses me softly.
His round, pale face reminds me of my mother's, the
moon, and a wheel of soft French cheese. He gently
makes love to me, every once in a while asking, "Is this
okay?" to which I reply, "Yes." Because it is okay. Not
great, but definitely okay.

On my way to the car the next morning, I run into a
girl I know from auditions.

"Girl, you are glowing. Hot night last night?!"

"Yeah, super hot! Kinda hot! Lukewarm. Ice cold. I'm not that sensitive to temperature, it's hard to know . . ."

"Well," she says, "enjoy that walk of shame."

I walk to the car with the warm sun on my back. Is it a walk of shame? I don't think I feel ashamed, but I do feel like I may be ready for a real relationship. And not because I'm so freaked out by the casual encounter. It's just, if I'm going to be having heinously boring sex, then I might as well have it with someone I love. And along with art house films and learning to cook, maybe one of our shared interests will be spanking. A girl can dream.

The Water Snake

Janie Haddad Tompkins

I had been modeling my life after a TV show. You
know the one. Four smart, funny single women who
were all looking for love and passion, but they also had
dream careers and out-of-reach Manhattan real estate.
God, I loved that show. No, not *The Golden Girls*. I
finished my MFA in acting, moved to Manhattan with
my fiancé, learned he was a sociopath leading a double
life, dumped him, and moved to Los Angeles as a single
woman—all during the first four seasons of *Sex and
the City*.

That show's influence led me to make a decision
when I was thirty-one to become a bona fide Casanova.
There isn't really a female term for being an adventurer
of *amore*, so maybe we'd call it being a "Samantha"
today?

I was tired of trying to have a meaningful relationship with a man. I wanted nothing to do with the opposite sex and trying to figure out what they wanted. I wanted to focus on what *I* wanted. And, at that time, what I wanted was a roll in the hay. No strings attached. I wanted to become a great lover, like a character in a French film or some erotica novel. I wanted to have a collection of perfumes and fringed silk scarves and have people say to me constantly, "God, Janie, you really should write your memoirs." And I would say, "Someday." Then I would stare off into the distance and say again, "Someday." And I wanted to do this overnight. So naturally, I turned to the Internet.

When a woman decides to have a one-night stand, it's complicated. First, you have to meet someone who is willing—and, in my experience, it was hard to find a guy who didn't want to stick around, especially if you didn't want him to. Second, when you're dealing with someone who is amenable to being your one-night sex toy, you have to be cautious about it—especially as a single gal living alone.

At least, that's what I heard you were supposed to do after I decided to become the Anaïs Nin of Beachwood Canyon. So I just stumbled across a stranger on MySpace. He looked decent enough in his photos and there was one of him and his dog. This was a plus since I'd read that serial killers start on animals and work up to something bigger. The living, breathing dog was affirming. There was another one of him at a friend's apartment party drinking a beer in baggy shorts and some kind of outdoorsy T-shirt. Seemed innocuous enough. We liked some of the same music, too. So I figured he was as good a candidate as any to pull into my web of seduction.

The flirtation began over the band REO Speedwagon. Well, actually, I had listed R.E.M. under my MySpace faves, but close enough for this particular endeavor. Back then, I would shamble home from my excruciating job waiting tables at a performance venue called M Bar and go deep into a social media rabbit hole as I glugged wine to cure the PTSD from my failed engagement. One Wednesday, this guy messaged me that I had good taste in music. His name was—well, I can't remember his name, so for the sake of the story, let's call him Tom. Note, however, he wasn't *the* Tom of MySpace; he was just a random dude who liked rock music.

To give you a sense of where I was exactly in my emotional journey toward sexual liberation, I'll say that after Tom pinged me, it took me two whole seconds to glance at his profile pictures and decide he would be in my boudoir by Friday night. I would conquer him. He would be mine. For one out-of-this-world, hair-tingling night.

I had him meet me at M Bar after my Friday night shift. I figured we had to have one drink in public first to at least earn a modicum of respectability. It was just for show; I had already planned to slip into a see-through tank top and silky tap pants when we got back to my apartment. I was at the bar under the flattering glow of the backlit liquor bottles, waiting to meet my blind hookup. He walked in, saw me, and immediately walked out.

Seconds later, my phone buzzed. It was Tom. He texted. "Oh my God, you're so cute." He came back in, smiling. He resembled his profile picture, except for being fifteen pounds heavier, which was totally workable for me. I was sticking to my plan, which was to have Tom sticking it to me in approximately forty-five minutes. It was late to begin with and I had a meeting the next morning so I needed to get this show on the road. But then I remembered that being a great lover means slowing down a little. Taking one's time. So I casually brushed my fingers against his as I reached over him for a cocktail napkin.

We ordered a drink and my friends were circling us like crazy, making sure this blind-date dude got the picture that I was loved and everyone knew exactly who I was with in case he was the Ted Bundy of Internet dating. I laughed about how cloying and protective they were being and suggested we go back to my apartment. He instantly agreed, and after he walked me to my car, we started making out against my passenger side door. Wow. I couldn't believe how easy this was all turning out to be. This was so in the bag. Done. Gathering a chapter for my memoirs. And I just knew it was going to be electrifying. Having sex with a stranger is a fantasy that I never thought I'd act out, but it was feeling so easy and giving me such a rush in my stomach, it was as though I had taken a hit of nitrous. I was having an out-of-body experience.

We got to my apartment and I poured us some wine, lit candles, and played some more dumb indie rock to impress him with my music collection. He liked to talk, but I shut him up by kissing him aggressively. I didn't really care what he had to say. I wanted to use him like a new mom uses baby wipes—extravagantly and with reckless abandon. As I got down to my skimpy nightwear, I unbuckled his belt and ripped down his pants and that's when I saw . . .

He was completely and utterly hairless from the waist down. As in, his dick and balls were shaved completely bald.

Since this was basically the first chapter of my memoirs, titled "Sex with a Guy on MySpace," I had never seen anything like this. I froze and stared. It looked like one of those water snake toys that you would get at the arcade. You know the ones, the slippery cylinders that you can't hold on to? Those ones that are little handheld plastic sheaths that encase some wiggly liquid and that slither out of your hand when you try to grip it? I stammered, "Oh my God, you have cancer."

"What?" he said.

"I mean," then hurriedly kissed him some more so I wouldn't have to look down.

"Wait, wait," he said as he pulled away. Then he leaned back and stuck it out. He waved down there with his hand, gesturing to his privates. "Do you like it?" he asked, referring to his alopecia of the nether regions.

So many things were going through my head. First of all, how does a guy even shave his testicles? I always thought men didn't want any harm to come to them, and to think of someone rubbing a razor blade dangerously close to his family jewels was perplexing. Secondly, the whole area was *so* closely shaved and hairless, I thought, *How many times a week does Tom have to shave them?* I mean, I get five o'clock shadow on my legs after three hours. Thirdly, he'd just asked me a question about his dick and balls—about whether or not I liked the shave job he'd done on them. I may be wrong about this, but it seems like when you are in an intimate moment with someone and they ask you whether you like something about them, especially when it refers to their genitals, you *are required* to say yes; there is no alternative. It's like when you're at someone's house for dinner and they serve gazpacho as the first course. Everyone knows cold soups are insanely stupid and unappetizing but you eat the gazpacho anyway for fear of offending the hostess and you most certainly coo that it's delicious.

I had a split-second decision to make. I didn't particularly love his shaved situation, since I was forced to be forming an opinion about it. I tend to gravitate toward manly types that don't overgroom and maybe even smell a little body-odor-ish. I am from the South, and no guy I had ever hooked up with south of the Mason-Dixon Line did anything like that south of *his* Mason-Dixon Line. And, no, that wasn't a line from *Sex and the City*—this was my actual real thought. I saw that I either had to become enthusiastic about Tom's extreme manscaping or fake a sudden migraine and go to bed frustrated and humiliated.

As I sat there covering up my stunned look by looking distracted, he asked again, "Do you like it?"

"Oh! Sorry, I thought I left the oven on for a minute. What? Oh! Yes. Do I like it? Yes! Tom, *yes*! It's . . . hot." I hoped he'd shut up about it and I could close my eyes through the rest of this so I could imagine more of a 1970s Burt Reynolds type instead of the newborn baby vibe he was going for. I attacked the closed-eye kissing again with a vengeance. Then he pulled away and said, "You should do it too; then it would feel really good when we are together."

I didn't let this comment land on me, as I couldn't even believe I was hearing this. When we were "together"? *This was a one-night stand*, I thought. *I am not a millennial—this is not how my relationships have ever started.* Once the one-night-stand card is played, there is no more calling afterward. I am from a generation where men give a customary "Last night was great" email and that's it. That's what I was signing up for! What was this "be together" thing, and especially, what was this "be together" in baldness thing?

I was offering up this passionate experience so freely, I hadn't even anticipated being given suggestions about my body appearance. It was getting unsexier by the second with Tom. But I went to an all-girls private high school that had the motto *Aut viam inveniam aut faciam* engraved on our senior rings. Roughly translated it means: *Where there's a will, there's a way.*

So I banged Tom and his bald balls as planned.

How I Might Have Just Become the Newest Urban Legend

Pamela Ribon

[WARNING: This story is not for the squeamish.]

At eight months pregnant, terrible things start happening. Things like: I could no longer feel my fingertips. The latter half of my pregnancy came with a double dose of carpal tunnel syndrome. It was best described as "shitty."

My gums bled when I brushed my teeth. I lost all the hair on my arms and an impressive amount of my eyebrows. I was eventually down to a single position in bed where I could sleep without my legs going numb. I caught a cold but wasn't allowed to take anything for it other than hot baths and pity parties. Not to mention the fact that there was a parasite living inside of me, absorbing all of my nutrients. Or, as my El Salvadorian housekeeper liked to say, "Your baby is stealing your beauty."

Then it got even worse. One week, I had to put my beloved sixteen-year-old cat to sleep. When I called my mom to cry to her about it, she told me about five other horrible things that were happening in my family. Then I got a call in the middle of that from my doctor to inform me that I had gestational diabetes.

Gestational diabetes is another wonderful thing that can happen to you when you're pregnant and your placenta hates you. In order to keep my baby from growing into a gigantic monster that couldn't possibly fit through my vagina, I had to go on a special diet and keep my blood sugars level. This meant I was testing my blood sugar by pricking my finger four times a day while eating the same boring, bland meals five times a day and I couldn't even sleep it off because sleep made my body go numb and then my husband went out of town and, during all of this, my cat was still dead.

Eventually I grew a bit cranky from eating saltines and string cheese for lunch while performing a blood-letting every four hours. Since I wasn't allowed scotch, my friend Cat suggested a nice, long massage. That sounded nice. Soothing.

We went to this place I'd been to a few times in my

neighborhood. It was no-frills, but tried to be serene and Namaste. It also had a coed quiet room where we were all forced to sit uncomfortably in robes waiting our turn, pretending we weren't a collection of strange and random men and women sitting together with nothing separating our naked bodies but robes and a pile of *InTouch* magazines.

This place didn't have individual rooms but rather a big room with tents that separated, like a dark fun-house. I never liked the separated tents because you ended up listening to someone else's massage and inevitably heard that one person who had no concept of other people—the one moaning, "Ungh! Yeah. That's it. Ooooooffffunh."

My masseur brought me to my section of tent and instructed me to take off my robe and climb up onto the table, Namaste-ing that he'd be right back. If you've never had a prenatal massage, basically they ask you to vault yourself onto a table that's taller than you're currently wide. Then you straddle a giant pillow while attempting to enjoy someone struggling to perform half a massage on each side of your awkward, bloated body. Imagine what one would need to do in order to hand-wash a whale, because it's a little like that.

I hauled myself up and managed to sort of shuffle-scoot between the sheet and the heavy blanket. And that's when I realized: I was wet.

I was wet, but also it was like I found a spot I somehow didn't dry off after I took my shower. But that wasn't possible, as I had showered more than fifteen minutes ago. It was dark in the room, and I was already on my side, so I kind of rubbed at where I was wet, which was all around my hips and butt. *This is kind of like a gel*, I thought. *Maybe I got into some lotion. But I don't know. I can't feel my fingers, so I'm not sure what I'm touching here. So maybe I'll just smell it.*

And it smelled like semen.

And that is because it was semen.

In case this has never happened to you, allow me to describe what happens next at this point. First of all, I'm sure natural instinct is to flip the fuck off that table. But it took me almost thirty seconds to even get into that position, and I was several feet off the ground, so there was no flinging my body anywhere. I opted to sort of sit up on my knees so I could investigate the fluid further, squinting to see in the dark, and I determined that yes, I was rolling around in a spunk puddle, but now it was on my hands and on my body and in front of me and—

And that's when my brain split in half and began trying to reason with itself.

"No, this can't be what is happening."

"It is. Try not to freak out, but you are covered in anonymous sperm."

"No, no. That's not. No, maybe we should just

lie back down and go to sleep. Maybe—maybe we're sleeping and this is all a dream!"

The masseur opened the curtain, getting a beautiful shot of my arched whale body, naked on my knees, giant tits and belly facing him. "Do you need more time?" he asked.

I stuttered, "Uh! Um . . . no, it's just . . . uh . . . there's something . . ." And I don't know what made me want to be polite in this situation, maybe it was the Enya or the romantic lighting, but mostly I was thinking of all the other people in their tents around me, even though instinct told me to scream, NO, I NEED YOU TO COME IN HERE AND DEAL WITH THE FACT THAT I AM COVERED IN JIZZ!

But instead I said, "Uh, there's something on the bed here and I'm . . . it's not . . . well, I think it's . . . from a man. Don't smell it."

That's the advice I gave out. "Hey, don't smell this. You're welcome."

So the masseur came in to investigate just as I pulled up the blanket to shield myself, but it was all over the blanket too because I'd been rolling around in it, so now it was just smeared all over me. I dropped the blanket and naked-flopped off the table. "I'm going to wash my hands while you . . . um . . . I think maybe I should wash my hands."

As the masseur inspected the sheets, some part of my

brain asked, *Wait, what if your water broke? What if that's all it is? Or just some kind of wet spot you made when you got on the bed? Or what if this is just another wondrous part of pregnancy?* Because you know how some of these women are. "When did you get your presperm? That's magical. I ate mine with my placenta."

So I was thinking, *What if this is all your fault and came out of you? Then you are going to feel like such an idiot.*

I went to inspect between my legs, but luckily some rational part of my brain screamed, *STOP! DO NOT TOUCH YOURSELF. WHILE YOU CAN'T GET PREGNANT AGAIN RIGHT NOW, DO YOU REALLY WANT TO STICK YOUR FINGER INSIDE YOURSELF CONSIDERING WHAT IT HAS JUST BEEN TOUCHING?* I am grateful for that part of my brain.

I washed my hands, and found Cat in the quiet area. I felt like I needed to do something. I whisper-stammered to her, "I don't . . . I don't really. Um. I need some advice." Like I was calling Martha Stewart. "Hi, I'm naked and covered in jizz. Club soda or . . . ?"

Here's how you know Cat's a good friend. When I told her what had just happened to me, she said, "Okay, well, that's disgusting and so we are leaving right now."

But here's how you know Cat's a great friend.

Because I then said, "Really? Man, I was kind of looking forward to a massage."

Cat didn't even bat an eye. She was just like, "Okay, yeah, then you're getting a massage. But you're getting a fucking great massage. Let's go talk to the manager."

We stormed up to the front area, which is not where people in robes were supposed to be, and as I quietly explained what happened, the masseur walked up, looking pale as hell. "Yeah, that guy who was just in there needs to be x'ed," he said. "It's everywhere in there. It soaked all the way through to every sheet."

Like he was describing a crime scene. "It's everywhere in there!" Which made me wonder what I would've seen if it hadn't been so dark in that tent.

The manager then explained how in the morning they layer twelve sheets on the massage tables. After each client leaves, they strip off a sheet or two and then move on. Somehow, this placated us. Cat and I had our hands on our hips, nodding, like, "Oh. Okay." All *CSI*. "Alright, then. As long as we know why this happened. Okay. Thanks."

The manager suggested I take a shower while they prepared a new room for me. I took a cold shower, trying to Silkwood myself, but mostly I was just thinking, *That sheet had not been changed. I was rolling around in Sperm Lake and this guy's trying to make me think this was two sheets down? No.*

The manager met me in the quiet room. "Again, so sorry," he whispered. "The owner isn't here, but after your massage, you and I can talk and we'll figure out what to do about the situation, but please just . . . try to enjoy your massage."

New table, new room, but I had the same masseur and he was mortified and I was mortified and it was awkward. I used that time to think about what to do, momentarily proud of myself for not running from that place screaming. I wanted to get my head straight to figure out my rights. That was all I could think to do. Somehow this must involve my rights, right?

So I was thinking, *Okay, I'm going to make sure we file an incident report, and we're going to sign things and agree on what happened and maybe I can get that guy's name so I can find out if he has . . . if he has any STDs because okay, I can't get pregnant, but, can I get syphilis? Hepatitis? At least one of the heps, right? That seems possible. What could I have maybe just given this baby? Do I need to call the doctors today? Will they make me get an emergency C-section because I'm a risk?*

Then I remembered that moments before I'd climbed up on that table of trauma I had given myself a blood sugar test. I had pricked my finger with a needle and bled on a stick. I'd given myself an open wound. And then used that same hand to scoop up some jizz and sniff it.

I was trying not to panic, but I was convinced I had just become an urban legend.

"Welcome to the wonderful world of AIDS!"

"Did you hear about the woman who got AIDS when she was completely alone?"

"Yes, did you know she also gave her baby AIDS? I never leave the house anymore because of that lady."

I was feeling very sorry for myself at this point. I also feel the need to mention that this guy was giving me a terrible massage. He was skipping around, not really doing any part that—well, now that I think about it, he skipped any part that had come in contact with the semen, which is smart, really, but he was half-assing it and sniffing constantly. I didn't want to open my eyes because I didn't want to find out that he was crying while rubbing my thighs, thinking about how he'd just given his last hand job in the back of this day spa now that this pregnant lady had ruined his life.

He abruptly stopped touching me and said we were done. I feel the need to mention that not only was the massage shitty and I'd thought about AIDS the entire time, but he'd also stopped it at thirty minutes instead of the full hour. The injustices just kept coming.

I was changing back into my clothes, trying to find privacy behind the sliver of my locker door, when the receptionist suddenly came up and grabbed me into a huge, no-warning hug. "You are a beautiful goddess creating life in your most special vessel," she said. Then she bit her lower lip in disgust. "I am so sick for you. I'm so insulted. Just mortified for you and your baby. I don't know how you're surviving." So I got away from her.

The manager took me to a back room that appeared to be half office, half supply room. He sat behind a desk next to a thick stack of blank gift certificates and said, "We don't really have anything in place for when something like this happens because something like this has never happened." I told him I wanted to file a report, adding that I'd like the client's name in case I ended up coming down with gestational herpes.

Was I supposed to call the cops? "Ma'am, can you describe the ejaculate that came into contact with your ridiculously pregnant body? Any distinguishing characteristics? Wait. Did you smell it? We maybe have somewhere to go if you smelled it."

The manager shifted in his seat. "Well, I don't think we can give you the client's name, but know that he's not allowed here anymore. We have his record, we can see his past history and anything he's done here before"—which made me think this had happened before—"but why don't you write down what happened and I'll email it to you and that way you have a record of it?"

"I don't need you to email me my own writing on what happened," I said. "That means nothing. I'm going to write a statement, you're going to write a statement, we're going to both sign it and then I'm going to call my doctors and see what we need to do next."

I was being very official, so I was kind of pissed that they weren't more appreciative of the fact that I wasn't just running through the quiet room screaming, "THIS PLACE IS MADE OF SEMEN!"

We wrote up our separate Word docs, but then his computer crashed so I had to get behind his desk to try to find the documents. But he hadn't saved them, so we had to write it all over again and then print it and sign it and I'd written this very detailed, very clinical version of events, trying not to use all-caps at any point. I'd written times and dates and my name and then I looked down and this guy had written: MALE CLIENT BEFORE PREGNANT LADY CLIENT EJACULATED EVERYWHERE AND SHE GOT IT ALL UP ON HER.

I mean, yeah, I guess that's all that happened.

I grabbed the cash I had in my wallet, which was like $12 or something, and I said, "This is all I have, but you can give it to the masseur."

The manager waved it away. "Please, ma'am, no. Of course you don't have to do that."

I very stoically put my money away, giving a quick nod of appreciation.

"We are just so sorry about this," he continued. "You're a loyal client and we'd hate to lose your future business over this, so just to make everything a little less stressful for you, and to apologize for things, we'd like to offer you a 50 percent discount on the massage you just had."

And I just went, "Well, no, I won't be paying that."

And he said, "Right, yes, of course."

Sometimes, when I think back over all this, the 50 percent discount is the biggest injustice of the entire story! And yes, I realize my thirty-minute shitty massage came with a free ass facial, but I still can't believe on any level that they thought I'd pay for this! If he didn't want to accept the tip is it because they knew that guy was jacking someone off right before I went in there?

WHY DO WE LET THINGS BE COED? WHY IS SPERM ALLOWED TO JUST BE WHEREVER?

I went outside to call my husband and immediately burst into tears, spitting out words like, "Semen man touching hips baby STDs whyyyyyy."

After he calmed me down, he asked, "You took a shower, right? Right after? Did you get it all?"

"I don't know!" I wailed. "I haven't been able to see nor touch 'it all' in quite some time!"

Cat met me outside after her massage. She said, "Yo, you know I Helen Kellered the shit out of my massage table before I got up there." She also mentioned that as a gay lady, she'd never been in contact with sperm before. "I wouldn't have known what it was. Pam, I might have been like, 'Oh, this must be a nice masque.'"

I called my OB/GYN and my doctor. But of course, I had to tell this story to each receptionist so she could tell the doctor. And I know these women have heard it all, but they hadn't heard this. I could tell by the way they were taking down notes. "Mmm-hm . . . and was this a massage parlor or . . . were you someplace . . . else?"

One receptionist was just like, "Girl, ew. We will call you back."

I couldn't wait for answers. I had to know my odds of dying, right then and there. I had to know if my baby was now bathing in diseased amniotic fluid. I had to know if I was the only person in the entire world and the history of people in it that this had happened to.

I'm a pretty good Googler. I can find most things on the Internet and get you an answer right away, but this one posed a particularly new challenge, as I couldn't really land on the right search words. And I can now tell you, without hesitation, that it's best never to Google "anonymous sperm on my ass."

The owner of the spa called to apologize, letting me know that they planned on changing how they did things in the tents, like having lights back there and maybe not doing the sheet thing. It seemed like the kind of thing where they should name the new, cleaner wing of tents after me: a giant plaque on the wall, perhaps.

THE PAMELA RIBON SPUNK-FREE PRENATAL MASSAGE ZONE. You're welcome, everybody.

"I'd rather not involve the police," the owner said. "I mean, it's not like the client broke the law, anyway, and I'm not sure what they can do."

Then one of the nurses called me back. "The doctor would like to know why you were rolling around on a table full of semen."

So I said, "Tell him that's not how I normally spend my Saturdays."

I called the L.A. County something-or-other that dealt with spas, and the guy acted like I was prank calling from a radio station. "We don't deal with that kind of stuff," he huffed. "We check pools and hot tubs. Whatever you do when you're in those rooms is at your own risk." Like there was nothing shadier than a prenatal massage.

My first doctor called back and couldn't even hide for a second that he was laughing. "Talk about an unhappy beginning! Ho ho ho!"

My other doctor just shrugged it off. "Look, you're probably fine. And besides, anything you could possibly contract from this won't show up for a couple of months, anyway."

Was that supposed to make me feel better?

I emailed the owner, trying to sound very stricken with grief, letting him know that the doctors had declared it "too soon to tell" and that I had concerns about the safety of his establishment. I casually mentioned how I'd recently bought gift certificates for some friends and now we were all too uncomfortable to use them. I dropped sixteen hints because—you guys, I don't know why I wanted him to offer me free massages for life, but it seemed like the only thing that made sense! Fuck Yelp; I could get on Facebook and contact the mega-mommies in my crazy neighborhood and that place would be shut down in seconds. But this guy hadn't even offered me anything in exchange for what I went through!

Where was the justice? Why didn't I get to just cum all over someone's day?

I confessed this story to a dear friend. After she finished being horrified, she also began laughing. "I'm sorry," she said. "But you really had an Ultimate White Lady Problem in that room—getting your feet rubbed, pan flutes playing, wondering if you just gave your baby AIDS through your butt."

I told her I was going to write about what had happened, because I still felt like I had to do something, even if it was just for closure. She said, "Just for a second, I'd like you to stop and think about whether or not you want this to be the legacy of your gestation. Do you really want to possibly be known forever as the Prenatal Massage Spunk Lady?"

And I realized: yes, I did.

And that is why you're reading this now. Because I have to believe that this all happened for a reason. When there's no recourse, nothing I can do—not even one free massage, damn it, that I might not have even used and if I did I certainly wouldn't tell anyone about it—I have to believe that this happened to make me do something loud and bold and brave. That yes, I was a beautiful vessel creating life, but I was also falling apart and in a lot of pain and I really couldn't feel my fingers and I had to think, I had to believe that this all happened because I was the chosen one, sent here to tell the world: LIFE IS GROSS. CARRY A FLASHLIGHT.

Dating

Rock Bottom

Cindy Chupack

ROCK BOTTOM: A low point, typically thought to require drugs or alcohol, but also achievable by singles who have "tried to be open-minded" a.k.a. "lowered their standards" to the point of almost no return.

The phone rings and wakes me. It's 6:15 AM Sunday morning in New York. Who would call at 6:15, I wonder. Maybe Rob, the married guy I've been seeing in Portland. I know you're not supposed to see married guys, by the way. I'm not proud of the fact that I was seeing a married guy. The thing is, every single woman, if she's single long enough, ends up in a relationship with a married guy. This includes men who don't tell you they're married when you meet them, men who tell you they're getting divorced, men who never plan to get divorced, and—in most cases—all three wrapped up in a handsome little package.

Now, women, God love them, have the amazing ability to believe these relationships might somehow work out, even though we are hard-pressed to find examples of this kind of thing working out, and we are bombarded (by friends and Dear Abby columns) with examples of this kind of thing not working out. Still, every woman who has ever dated a married guy has believed that she is different. That this is love. That this was meant to be, and the timing was just off by a few years and possibly some kids. You see, for single women, the fairy tale is ever-evolving, and when you think you're in love, you can figure out a way to make the fairy tale include a married guy. It's part of our charm and part of our downfall.

Of course, my "affair" if it must be called that (I would prefer to call it my "derailment") ended exactly the way these things are supposed to end, with Rob realizing how much he loved and cherished his family, and me realizing that even though you go through life thinking you are in your own movie, occasionally you realize you've stumbled into someone else's movie, and you are not, in fact, Julia Roberts. At best you're one of the Arquette sisters—in for an act or two, a catalyst for someone else's story. Things will not necessarily end happily for you. Your character may not even learn a lesson.

But the morning the phone woke me I was drowsy and deluded, and I still thought I was Julia Roberts.

The phone rings again. How can it be Rob? It's only 3:15 in Portland.

Me: Hello?

Rob: I can't sleep. *(He sounds weird, troubled.)*

Me: Is something wrong?

Rob: What are you doing?

Me: Talking to you.

Rob: What are you wearing?

Me: Flannel pajamas. *(I laugh.)* Not very sexy, huh? What are you wearing?

Rob: A shirt and nothing else. Take off the bottoms.

Me: Really?

Rob: Yeah.

Me: . . . Okay. (I'm thinking about how I recently told Rob, when he was feeling like a creepy guy for falling for someone while he was married, that he wasn't a creepy guy, that creepy guys drive flashy sports cars and buy their girlfriends lingerie and have phone sex. Is that why he's doing this—because he's feeling like he made his creepy bed, he might as well lie in it?)

Rob: Unbutton the top.

Me: . . . Okay.

Him: Now show me your lips.

Me: (I briefly think, *He wants me to smile? Oh,*
   those *lips.* This is weird. Rob doesn't talk like
   that, although we've never had phone sex before. Maybe he's trying to be kinky, and he's
   just not very good at it.)

Him: Tell me to lick your pussy.

Me: (*weakly*) Lick my pussy. (Wait a minute! What
   if this isn't Rob?)

Him: Now what do you want me to do?

Me: (I could be talking to a stranger! A weirdo! I
   should hang up! But what if it *is* Rob trying to
   be sexy and I hang up on him? Maybe I should
   say, "Who is this?" No, because if it *is* Rob,
   won't he think that's odd since I was already
   playing along? My solution is to laugh and say
   . . .) Hey, Rob, how do I know this is you?

Him: (*pause*) It's me.

Me: (Despite the early hour, I come up with) What
   T-shirt do I have of yours?

Him: (*long pause*) The black one.

Me: That's right! (But it could have been a lucky
   guess.) What does it say?

Him: You tell me.

Me: No, you tell me.

Him: (*long pause*) How do you like my big hard
  cock!

That is not what the T-shirt says. I hang up. I call
Rob's cell, hoping it was him, hoping we'll laugh about
how I thought it could have been anybody else. He
doesn't answer. Of course he doesn't answer! It's 3:15
there! He and his wife are asleep! A glimmer of hope—
maybe he was drunk! Which would be bad, because
he's a recovered alcoholic, but it still seems better than
the alternative—that I just took off my flannel pajamas,
even apologized because they weren't sexier, and said
"Lick my pussy" for some New York wacko I thought
was my married boyfriend! I hope he'll call back. That
Rob will call back. No one calls. Not Rob. Not the
wacko.

You'd think at least the wacko would call back.
I was certainly a good sport. I am at once mortified
and insulted. I look up at the ceiling. I look up at rock
bottom.

The Kid

Sara Benincasa

I stood alone in the middle of his dorm room at 8:00 AM, stark naked, eyes wide. The fire alarm was blaring, and I could hear the sound of footsteps as residents rushed down the hall. An RA pounded on his door, shouting that this wasn't a drill but a real fire. And all I could think was, "Sara Benincasa! You are thirty-one years old. You are *too old* to die in a dorm fire!"

I don't make a habit of sleeping with university students. If I did, I'd probably pick a graduate student. (My host that evening was not a graduate student.) If I had to go with an undergraduate, I'd at least pick a senior. (He was not a senior.) But the gentleman whom I'll call Junior (for that is what he was) had just turned twenty-one the previous month. And he was very cute and very nice, and very much a part of my one-third-life crisis.

I called it a one-third-life crisis because I think it's reasonable to expect that because I don't drink too much and I don't smoke and I think about going to the gym, I might live until the age of ninety-three. I'm not Methuselah and I'm not going to live until my 120s so it wasn't a quarter-life crisis and it wasn't a midlife crisis because I want to live past my sixties. So there's the math on that.

The past couple of years had been a bit dramatic. There had been a layoff from a job in radio, a job where I spent three hours each weeknight giving love and sex advice to strangers from around the country. There had been a subsequent downturn in my finances. There had been a relationship with a man I suspected could be the love of my life, and then there had been a breakup. The breakup was followed shortly thereafter by a relationship with a soldier, and then the soldier was deployed to Afghanistan. Unsurprisingly, the romance did not survive the distance. And because I'd never dealt with the breakup with the aforementioned possible love of my life, my breakup with the soldier opened up a space for the mourning of not one but two relationships.

I drank a lot that year.

I also had a higher-than-usual (for me) amount

of sex with a higher-than-usual (for me) amount of partners. I'm a stand-up comedian, so I'm always surrounded by male stand-up comics. Trying to have sex with one of these gentlemen is roughly as difficult as shooting already-dead fish in a small barrel with an AK-47. I did not lack potential partners. I even had sex with a female friend, which was figuratively and literally a stickier experience than our usual activity of choice: chatting over coffee.

I met Junior when he contacted me via Facebook to ask me if I would host his birthday party. As a stand-up comic, I get requests like this. But he could only pay me in free drinks, he said.

"Oh, how old are you turning?" I asked pleasantly.

"Twenty-one."

Oh, Lord. The last thing in the world I wanted to do was host some privileged Ivy League kid's twenty-first birthday party. I had better things to do. Thankfully, I was already booked that night.

Then I looked at his photos on Facebook.

And then I remembered that I was really lonely and that I hadn't been in therapy for a few months so I said, "Hey, I can't host your party, but I can take you out for a belated birthday drink later that week."

"Cool!" he said, and that's how we met up a few days later.

He was a musician, *of course*—there's really no point

in fucking a twenty-one-year-old boy who doesn't have a marketable skill. While twenty-one-year-old girls are ripe for fucking regardless of their talent or expertise, twenty-one-year-old boys are different. They need some redeeming quality to partly make up for the fact that they are twenty-one-year-old boys.

The evening progressed as these nights usually do: we had dinner, we had drinks, we had more drinks, we had to take a walk to my apartment so we could watch music videos on my laptop, we had to go to my bedroom so I could show him my vagina, etc. The sex was the kind of sex that you have when you're twenty-one—you just sort of stick one thing in another and hope the condom doesn't break. But it was fun and we both decided that it should happen again. So it did, on another occasion. And then another time, followed by another time.

Pretty soon we weren't just fucking—we were *hanging out*. We were going to bars. We were going to parties *with other people*.

It is a terrible but inevitable truth that when you date someone born in the early to mid 1990s, you will eventually have to meet his friends. Have *you* ever tried to have a conversation with a group of people born in the early to mid '90s? What do you say, really? Well, let me tell you. You say things like, "Oh, let me tell you about the first Clinton administration." Or: "*Full*

House? Oh, it's a show that was on when you were a baby."

I would sit there with these kids who were so nice and sweet and I would have on a ton of foundation—I'd really spackle that shit on to cover up any crow's-feet that might be peeking through—and I would be wearing some cute outfit from Forever 21 because I was telling myself that that's what I was and they would ask me questions like, "What year are you?" And I would have to say, "Oh . . . I graduated." I did not want to add ". . . from graduate school when you were a sophomore."

Through this relationship, I came to understand something that had eluded me before. See, I used to get so mad when the men I knew would date much younger women. I have a lot of male friends who are stand-up comedians in their thirties and forties and these men would, if they could, just date fetuses. They would date a zygote even; put hot pants on a zygote and these men would fuck it. And these guys were horrified that I was dating a twenty-one-year-old. They would say things like, "What are you doing? This is ridiculous! He's twenty-one. What can he offer you?"

I would respond, "Well, *he* has health insurance." (Granted, it was also his parents' health insurance, but I had a point. Kind of.)

But I came to understand something unexpected. I always used to wonder why it was that men dated younger women and I'd ask myself, "What is it they're doing? Are they trying to recapture their youth?" And I learned the answer.

Yes. Yes, they are.

Because there's this thing that happens when you're with a much younger person: you think that maybe somehow, some way, you can just absorb their youth and take it into you like some kind of vampire. You think that perhaps you can suck in all that self-worth and confidence and innocence and adorable belief that life holds something worthwhile. And maybe, just for a moment, you think, you can have that, too.

And then you go home and you look at yourself and your life and you realize you're not in a dorm room— that you're a grown-up who can't pay your bills.

At least that's what you realize if you're me.

Another problem was my parents. I talk to my parents about a lot of stuff so they knew that I'd been on this kind of wild fuck spree, just sort of dealing with my feelings by humping things. And so at one point when Junior and I had started to see each other regularly, they asked me if I was still seeing a lot of guys.

I answered, "No, I'm seeing just one guy." They were so excited. So I added, "Yeah, he's Italian, too— like we are."

They echoed, "Italian!"

Then I said, "And he's Catholic, too."

And they just got more excited and said, "Catholic!"

So I continued, "And he lives in the city."

They asked, "Does he have a job?"

That's when I hesitated. "He's studying history."

A pause, and then, "Oh, he's in graduate school. Where does he go?"

"He *is* in school," I said slowly. "It's his third year."

"Oh, is it a PhD program?"

And finally I just said, "No, it's not a PhD program. Actually, he's twenty-one."

I don't think I've ever disappointed my parents so much. In their head, I was dating a sexy but wizened older professor on a tenure track of some kind. But no, I was with a mere child.

My girlfriends were also freaked out, but one of them, a wealthy lawyer, decided to give him a chance. She took us out for a fancy dinner one night after one of my comedy shows. Junior looked at the table with awe.

"Cloth napkins," he whispered to me.

"Just act normal, please," I hissed back.

My friend ordered us a bottle of wine, most of which she polished off. Then she began tearfully recounting what she was undergoing in an effort to get pregnant and lamenting that she hadn't frozen her eggs. These were the kinds of dates I would take him on.

"It's just like, I don't even know if I should do IVF,"

she sniffled, dabbing at her eyes. "It's so hard, you know what I mean?" She looked at him plaintively, and he nodded comfortingly. And he was just so sweet about it. I remember him sitting there and saying, "You know what? Sometimes it just takes time. Your husband loves you, you love your husband, and that's what matters. And so what if you do have to do IVF? That's cool! Some of my friends are IVF babies."

Of course it ended. I needed to find someone my own age, and he needed to go to South by Southwest with his indie folk fusion band. These things happen.

But we've stayed in touch via Facebook, occasionally checking in on each other's progress in life and in career or, um, school. He's a senior now, writing his thesis. I ran into him in New York recently, and we chatted about it.

"Writing a thesis is the hardest thing in the world," he said.

"What's it about?"

"The history of the role of women in classical Greek and Roman societies," he replied.

"Sounds fascinating," I said.

"It is."

We smiled at one another pleasantly.

And then he said to me, with no trace of irony, "I'm just really into ancient women."

The Older Man

Anna Davies

I went to high school during the late nineties, when *Sex and the City* was still sexy, when "chick-lit" wasn't a pejorative term, and when the girl power movement made dating seem like a cross between a game of Candy Land and a Choose Your Own Adventure book—and the only losers were the ones who weren't brave enough to explore all their options. As soon as I began actual *dating* dating—which, to me, meant meeting a man you didn't know from years of attending the same school, not splitting the bill, and occasionally ending the evening with an X-rated sleepover—I approached it like a serious scavenger hunt. In my mind, it was optimal—no, essential—that I have plenty of experiences with as many different types of guys as possible (and a few women) so that I could truly *know* that no stone had been left unturned before I finally settled down.

Part of that mentality was spurred by my career. I worked as a writer and editor focusing on love and relationships, and many editorial meetings with my boss ended up being discussions about my dating life in the hopes they could be used for a feature story. And this is perhaps why I didn't mind that the majority of my "relationships" were short-lived flings with guys who could have been sent straight from central casting to fit neatly into broad categories that define the stereotypical single city girl's romantic partners: the Coke-Addicted Wall Street Banker, the Aspiring Brooklyn Musician with a Mustache, the C-List Celebrity with the Impressive Apartment, the Nerdy but Brilliant Guy with Mommy Issues, the French Guy Who Is Equally Amazing at Cooking and Oral Sex. If nothing else, they all made for awesome stories.

By the time I was twenty-eight, I'd checked off most of the categories—except one. I'd never dated an older man. Sure, I'd gone out with guys who were a decade or so older than me, but never with an old-enough-to-be-your-father, clear-to-everyone-around-you-that-you're-dealing-with-daddy-issues old dude.

Which was why I was intrigued when I met Eugene. (No, that's not his real name. But his real name is one that screams *born prior to 1960.*) He was a former coworker of a friend's boyfriend and hosted a summer barbecue that my friend invited us to. I brought a bag of chips and was surprised when the address my friend gave led me to an actual Manhattan townhouse in the middle of a sunny, tree-lined downtown block. None of my friends lived in *houses.* For that matter, some of my friends didn't even live in bedrooms but in a corner of a living room that had been subdivided by a sheet. I glanced down at the bag of chips purchased from the corner bodega, sure I'd gotten the wrong address.

Just as I was about to text my friend, the door swung open, leaving me face-to-face with a silver-haired man wearing wire-rimmed glasses who looked to be in his mid-sixties.

"You must be Beth's friend. Come in!" he announced. Dubiously, I stepped across the entrance, noting the leather couches, the original art, the hardwood floors covered with expensive-looking rugs. I glanced from my bag of chips to my flip-flops to my cutoff jean skirt. Why hadn't Beth told me this was a *grown-up* party?

The man's gaze followed my own.

"I brought chips," I said as I unnecessarily thrust the bag toward him.

"Thank you." He ushered me through room after room until we got to the back patio. A bubbling marble fountain stood in the center, while smaller fountains framed by brightly painted marble tiles adorned the stone walls. Jazz music played softly in surround sound. A cheese tray and fruit slices were laid out on a table surrounded by only two couples.

Beth glanced up.

"Hey," she said casually. I glared at her, trying to telepathically ask her why she didn't let me know that this wasn't the hipster-filled, beer-soaked bash I'd been expecting.

As the night got later and the second bottle of $300 wine was poured, I realized that Eugene may have been old and wealthy, but he could still tell dirty jokes and bitch about the dating scene. He didn't just listen to jazz, he also went to Daft Punk concerts. By the end of the evening, I was intrigued . . . and wondering if he was the perfect candidate to fill the role of older, wealthy suitor.

So I sent him a handwritten thank-you note and dropped it in the mail the next day, adding my email address to the bottom of the card. He emailed back, thanking me and wondering if I'd like to meet for dinner at Nobu, the swanky TriBeCa sushi restaurant.

It was *such* a cliché suggestion—and I loved it. I instantly responded yes, noting that he, like most people in my parents' age group, had an AOL email address.

As I got off the subway at seven that Friday, I

received a text: "Already got here. I told the hostess to look for the woman with the beautiful red hair."

Ugh. Not only was that over-the-top, it was also incorrect. I'd dyed my hair back to brown since he'd seen me. I slunk over to the hostess booth.

"I'm here with Eugene," I mumbled, steeling myself for the side-eyed glance that came seconds later. She clearly thought I was a prostitute. I smiled and shrugged, wanting her to understand that this wasn't something I did all the time, that it was a *sociological experiment.*

He ordered for us and we talked about our lives. We didn't have much in common, and I found that I was constantly flitting in between extremes, playing sophisticated, worldly world traveler one moment as I talked about my career, then playing whiny teenager the next when he tried to make me try a piece of sashimi I already knew I was going to hate. I noticed the waiters asking him if I needed another drink. And I definitely noticed a few glances in our direction from other diners assessing the situation.

After dinner, he asked me if I wanted to go back to his place, and of course I agreed. At that point, even the awkwardness was a turn-on. I *liked* the fact that people were gossiping about us, imagining me as some sort of call girl or gold digger. That persona seemed way more interesting than who I really was. I also liked the way he paid attention to me, which was different than most first dates with men in my own age group, who'd often ask a question only so they could answer it themselves when I finished speaking.

Once we got back to his house, we started making out on the couch, which wasn't any different than any other make-out session I'd had in the past. In fact, it felt like making out was simpler than talking. In the moment, we were a man and a woman on a date, assessing physical chemistry.

The problem came when he actually spoke.

"I really want to make love to you," he whispered in my ear. I cringed. Who *made love* anymore? People in my generation do something that rhymes with "truck." That word made me excited. "Making love" made me feel awkward and embarrassed. Which was why I kissed him more forcefully, then looked into his eyes.

"Let's go upstairs," I suggested.

Once we were in the bedroom, he gave me a brief tour. It's one of those oddities I've found often occurs in first encounters—the action is momentarily interrupted for a "look at my stuff!" show-and-tell session. With guys my own age, it's usually his favorite Spotify playlist. Eugene showed me his sock drawer. Or, more particularly, the $30,000, mostly in small bills, wedged in between rolled-up balls of dark-hued socks.

"I won it in Vegas," he explained. "I like to keep it here just so I have cash when I need it."

Seriously? I was lucky to scrounge together a dollar from my drawer, but he had the equivalent of more than half my salary. It was disgusting and showy . . . and kind of turned me on.

I reached down. His penis was hard. That was unexpected—I'd heard enough horror stories about guys having trouble getting it up once they hit their forties— but that wasn't the only hard thing about the hookup. Being aware of the age gap made me automatically try to keep any dirty talk out of the conversation and also made me overly on the lookout for any potential heart attack symptoms. He had a *Why would you do that to yourself?* reaction to my tattoo. And as I tried to fall asleep in his arms, I couldn't stop staring at the framed photo of his two twenty-something daughters smiling back at me.

The next day he emailed. And emailed again. And emailed again, until I had six emails piled up in my inbox in a twelve-hour span of time. The first one was a general *I had a lovely time and would like to see you again. Let's do Thursday?* The last one was to-the-point, bare-faced bribery.

Would you like an iPod?

I blinked at the email, visions of the $30K in his sock drawer dancing in my head. Once I got over the initial annoyance that my affections, to him, were worth an iPod, I was almost charmed by his complete lack of game. Clearly, he wasn't trying to impress me—he just didn't know how to connect with someone who was born during the Reagan administration. So I decided to give him the benefit of the doubt and go out with him again . . . and again.

I ended up dating Eugene for a month, including another barbecue, where he occasionally pulled me into the kitchen to make out with me while his twenty-something personal trainer, clearly aware of what was going on, gave me the side-eye. There were some things I genuinely liked about the experience: he had good manners and he made it obvious from his numerous emails that he liked me, which was affirming. And on the shallow end, I really enjoyed trying expensive restaurants around the city. I also loved sliding into the passenger seat of his BMW as he drove back to his house, and I loved the hour or so after, where he'd sit on a patio bench and I'd lie with my head in his lap and look up at the stars. It was in those conversations that he'd bring up the future and ask if I could see us getting serious and talk about how he thought he'd want to try marriage and parenthood again and this time, do it right.

In those moments, in the murky twilight, I imagined what it would be like. It would be so easy: never having to worry about money again. Not having to keep going on dates. Having someone else who I could actually depend on, unlike the many guys I'd dated, who had enough trouble taking care of themselves. Of course, his daughters would likely hate me and all the other parents at our potential child's preschool would gossip about me but *it could be a possibility.*

Old Guy Eugene didn't see me as a twenty-something wide-eyed woman—he saw me as an actual person he wanted in his life.

I broke up with him.

I felt bad afterward, wondering why I couldn't be more open-minded. We'd had some good conversations. He actually bought and read the books I'd written. He planned dates he thought I'd like and always opened the door for me. Dates I could discuss with friends or dissect in a story ideas meeting were one thing, but turning it into something real? I couldn't do that. I knew, deep down, that even though I'd never accepted the iPod or the vacations or asked for any of the cash that was just a few feet away when I slept over—I was still being materialistic. It was just that *he* was my material.

And of course, the subsequent moral is neat, concise, and sitcom-ready: he may have been old, but he was the one who made me grow up.

Before you can gag, let me be clear: I am not a chick-lit heroine, and learning a lesson and following it are two different things. So even though *date an older wealthy dude* is crossed off the list, I'm still curious about plenty of other situations.

Speaking of which, can you introduce me to any politicians?

The Clown

Sara Barron

The other week I was waiting for the subway at Union Square. It was late at night and I was reading *The New York Times*, which, for me, always means I'm in a position to be easily distracted. Concentrating on world affairs is always something I feel I *should* do, which means I *do* do it, but only occasionally and always poorly. So I was people-watching and glancing intermittently around the station when all of a sudden I caught the eye of a man in a clown outfit. He winked at me and started walking in my direction. I'm not usually the type to talk to strangers—especially one in a red foam nose who initiates an interaction with a wink—but this guy looked really familiar, which piqued my interest because it's not like I know all that many working clowns in the city. You'd think if I saw one who looked familiar, my next thought would be, *Oh, right . . . that guy.* But that was not the case. I knew I knew him and I couldn't figure out how, so I decided to say hello and he, a well-mannered clown, said hello back.

"I think we've met before," I said. "Remind me of your name."

He bowed then and did a *ta-da!* with his hands before saying, "I'm Mr. Clown!"

It was a spectacular introduction, so I laughed and said, "All right, 'Mr. Clown.' But what's your *real* name?"

I expected a reply along the lines of "Don't you remember?" I'd be embarrassed and shake my head no and he'd continue, "I'm so-and-so! From such-and-such! Well, I'm a street performer now!" Then we'd have a laugh, talk about how much time had passed, exchange numbers, and make an empty promise to catch up over coffee.

But instead Mr. Clown said again, "I'm Mr. Clown!"

So *again* I asked his real name.

"I just told you: Mr. Clown. That is my real name."

"Well, I don't believe you," I told him.

He shrugged. "You don't have to believe Mr. Clown; it's still my real name."

Talking in the third person is even more bizarre than titling oneself a clown in my opinion, so I shouted, "Who are YOU?! Now answer, 'I am . . .'"

"... MR. CLOWN!"

The other people on the subway platform started taking notice as I racked my brain for more specific possibilities.

"Are you Josh Green?" I asked. "From Sunset Woods Day Camp?"

"Nope."

"Sam Feinzimer?"

"Nope."

"Are you from Chicago? New York? Did we go to school together?"

My gut instinct was that I'd seen him naked at some point in the last decade, but I couldn't be too sure, so I continued listing names: "Danny Levinson?"

"I *am* Mr. Clown!"

"Justin Rubenstein?"

"I *am* Mr. Clown!"

After five minutes he tired of our back-and-forth and excused himself by heading to the nearest, fullest garbage can. "I need new props," he said, and rummaged through until he found a Poland Spring bottle, a Coke can, and a container of baby powder.

"Watch this!" he declared. "I can juggle!"

For me, voluntary contact with garbage and dementia are tightly intertwined. The sight of the rummaging knocked me out of my trance of frustration and I thought, *So you're mistaken. He's not someone you know; he just looks like he is.* But then once I'd found the wherewithal to turn to go, he taunted me with, "Why are you leaving so soon . . . SARA . . . BARRON?"

One thing I knew for sure was that I hadn't given him my name. "WHO *ARE* YOU?!" I bellowed.

"MR. CLOWN!" he answered back. "It was lovely seeing you again!" And with that, he waved goodbye and boarded the oncoming train.

I hate surprises and I hate games that involve guessing; it's the powerlessness of it all that turns me off. So when a clown in a subway proves he knows me but won't tell me how or why, I get manic. I ran out of the station and splurged on a cab back to my apartment so Mr. Clown could be immediately Googled. I tried a few advanced search combinations of "Mister" versus "Mr.," which led me to a list of actor bios in a quintuple-Off Broadway production entitled *A Forest Made of Dreams*, which in turn led me to the name Daniel Stewart.

I just about fell off my chair when I read that name.

Daniel Stewart was my boyfriend for a month in 1998, the summer after my freshman year of college when I stayed in New York and worked as an usher at the Lucille Lortel Theatre in the West Village. He worked there, too—we worked adjacent aisles—and within a week of meeting, we'd begun spending much of our free time together in his mother's Park Slope brownstone, either watching TV or engaged in rounds of oral sex. After a month I went home to Chicago for the remainder of the summer and we lost touch. Working together six days a week, we'd never gotten around to actually exchanging numbers, and it seemed we'd been lost to each other for good. In the six years that followed, I'd remembered him fondly: when you date someone just for a month and keep it simple with reruns of *Three's Company* and the aforementioned oral sex, when all that tears you apart is circumstance, it's easy to keep the gent up on a pedestal. That's where Daniel Stewart was for me, the individual conveniently referred to when other relationships went awry, when I got asked to pee by an acting student or dissed by a hand model. That's when I'd think, *You know who I clicked with? Daniel Stewart. He was fun. One day we'll meet again, I bet, in a cozy coffee shop or wine bar, and give it a second go. Unmarred by my traveling schedule or his mother in the adjacent bedroom scatting along to Cab Calloway albums, our romance will take flight!*

Great reunions like this take time, and I had prepared to wait. I just hadn't prepared for the clown costume or the foam nose and rainbow wig obscuring his identity. Nor had I prepared to see said rainbow wig featured in his online headshot.

Perusing the website for *A Forest Made of Dreams*, I realized the show was still playing and I debated whether or not I ought to go to see it. The moment felt very Choose Your Own Adventure:

You realize your former flame has gone crazy!
Do you:

A. Keep the past in the past and spend Friday night on the couch nursing your soup in a cup?
   Or

B. Douse your face in tinted moisturizer, then hit the town running in your best attempt to track him down?

I chose B. After our conversation in the subway, it wasn't so much that I cared to try to reignite the romance, it's more that I felt desperate to know what had happened. How did Daniel Stewart become Mr. Clown? When was the breaking point? What prompted it? Which medications were tried? Did drug use play a part? Also, could I change him back? If yes, fantastic, and so could begin Part Two of our epic romance. If not, well, that would be less fantastic but at least I'd have some answers to my questions. I knew it would be bold just randomly showing up at his show, but the thing about a man devoted to his clown persona is that it makes him seem all at once vaguely dangerous by virtue of his apparent unhingedness but also less intimidating. (While you can fear a clown, you're not necessarily worried what he thinks about you.) So I packed a bottle of NoDoz and a can of mace—to keep me awake during the show and to protect me once it finished—and ventured to this basement theater space on Manhattan's Lower East Side.

A Forest Made of Dreams featured Mr. Clown in the role of Hans Morganstern, a lumberjack who aspires to a future made of something more than chopping wood. The text was written entirely in verse, an ABAB rhyme scheme that included phrases like:

> There's so much more than this to see!
> So much pain in the 'hood!
> What is wanted from me?
> I'll go chop some more wood!

It lasted a merciless two and a half hours, and at the end of it I waited for Daniel—or was I supposed to call him Mr. Clown?—outside the front door of the theater. It would've been impossible to play my presence off as a random coincidence, so free as I was from worry about his judgments or looking like a stalker, I explained myself honestly.

"So! Hello again!" I said. "I have to admit, I Googled you after our run-in the other day, just because I was like, 'Ahh! Who is that guy?' And anyway, well, I guess I figured it out . . . Daniel." His face twitched when I said "Daniel." "Can I call you Daniel?"

"You can call me whatever you want," he answered, "but understand that now I'm Mr. Clown."

The "now I'm Mr. Clown" seemed promising in comparison to the more adamant "I *am* Mr. Clown," and this encouraged me to keep the conversation going. I asked if he had any plans and, if not, might he like to go and get a beer. "I'd love to catch up," I said, "and hear what you've been up to. Since, you know, it seems like you've got . . . a lot . . . going on."

He told me he refused to frequent bars, and when I asked him why he explained, "Because people in bars always laugh at me."

I pointed out that he was dressed like a clown.

"My intention is to be laughed with, never at," he went on. "A clown—*this* clown—should not be a joke, but rather a source of inspiration."

"For *what*?" I asked. And then, fearing I'd sounded counterproductively hostile, I said, "Well, what I mean to say is, what are you hoping to inspire?"

"The gifts of hope and love and laughter."

I'm adept at one-upping people's craziness. Talk to me about the gifts of hope and love inherent in your clowning, and I'll happily outdo you with some anecdote regarding the imaginary friends I had when I was six, the ones I'd talk to only when I moved my bowels. In this conversation, however, I decided I'd let Daniel wear the crazy crown, focused as I was on working out the how and why of his persona. Also, I enjoyed feeling like the normal one for once. I nodded like a gal considering a valid point. "Wow," I said. "What an interesting perspective."

Mr. Clown suggested that instead of a beer in a bar, we go for a walk. "It *would* be nice to catch up," he admitted. "And being outdoors feels safer to me."

To him, sure. But what about the girl on the quasi-date with the full-time clown? It *was* Friday night on the Lower East Side, however, and the streets were packed with hordes of revelers and vomiters and cops and homeless folks, and all this commotion made me feel safe too, I guess, like maybe I wasn't on the verge of a payback for all the date-rape jokes I'd ever made.

Mr. Clown and I began our walk up toward Alphabet City. I asked questions while we walked, and he gave long, circuitous answers that never circled back to asking me what I was up to. This was just as well, seeing as how my work in retail sales wasn't something I ever felt compelled to talk about. I learned Daniel Stewart had "disappeared" in 1999, not long after we'd last seen each other. After finishing college upstate, he returned to his mother's brownstone, at which point he was overtaken with an all-encompassing malaise: What should he do with his life? Who was he *really*? Was this all there was? What could he do to make a difference? To really *be* somebody? Then one day he took his five-year-old niece to see the Barnum & Bailey Circus at his mother's urging. Watching all the clowns skip happily around in oversized pajama pants, squirting each other with water-rigged daisies, he realized "clowning was the key to joy." He enrolled in a clown college in San Francisco and emerged two years later as Mr. Clown.

"Why 'Mr. Clown'?" I asked.

"Because I am a man," he answered. "*And* I am a clown."

He never broke from this persona, removing the foam nose only to shower and sleep, responding only to the title Mr. Clown, exhibiting a long-term level of commitment with a graceful bit of tattooed calligraphy sprawled across his lower back that said, THE CLOWN IS LOVE. I know that's what it said because he showed me.

"I owe the clown my life," he said. "And so I give the clown my life."

Whether thanks to Stephen King's *It* or John Wayne Gacy's face paint, a lot of people fear clowns, but I've always kept my associations less complex and menacing. I think first of balloon animals and oversized lips. I was poised to find Mr. Clown's company delightful or at least amusing, but the more we walked and talked, I just got to feeling depressed. "Clown" meant joy and laughter to Daniel Stewart, but now to me, it just meant slaughtered hopes for romance and a blatant manifestation of my own insensitive and exploitative tendencies. Daniel had gone a form of crazy that seemed to surpass entertaining and land on tragic, and here I was motivated by wanting sex or romance, or at least a laugh at his expense. The disappointment and self-loathing got me feeling short of breath, which made me crave a shot of amaretto. Well, there'd be no amaretto at a bar with Mr. Clown, which was how and when and why I figured it was time for us to go our separate ways.

When we reached Union Square, the site of our reunion, I braced for an awkward goodbye. I imagined a 24/7 clown didn't log much time with the ladies, and by simple virtue of not having shied away from his persona, I automatically presumed I'd be asked out for another walk or approached for a kiss. I was preparing a sensitive rejection when he suggested we kill some time on a nearby park bench. "My girlfriend's on her way, but she won't be here for a bit," he said. "Wanna sit and wait?"

For seventy-two hours I'd been consumed by the question "What happened to Daniel Stewart?" Well, that flipped in an instant to "Who *dates* Daniel Stewart?" I expected a bearded lady or one-armed ventriloquist, but five minutes later a shockingly beautiful Bolivian woman arrived. In timid, accented English she muttered, "Oh. Hall-oooo," while grabbing Daniel's hand. She was normal by all outward appearances, and she cuddled against him as he encouraged me to come to the back car of the R train some weekday afternoon to check out his juggling show, a performance he described as much more "me" than *A Forest Made of Dreams*.

I said I would but knew I wouldn't and watched as he put his arm around his girlfriend and escorted her away.

As the clown and the Bolivian got smaller in the distance, I wondered who my other half might be. Daniel Stewart had been the default face on this otherwise ambiguous fantasy for years; what vision should replace him? If the standards in New York are such that a clown gets an ESL-ed stunner, what was I to hope for? I figured it best to keep my options open and scanned the streets for any man without a wig.

The Test

Chellis Ying

*T*hat Monday, I woke up to a call from my gynecologist. "Your test results are back and they showed up positive for chlamydia," she said.

"What?"

"Chlamydia is a sexually transmitted disease."

She said this as if I'd never heard of it before, but of course, I knew what chlamydia was. Along with herpes, gonorrhea, AIDS: these are the things that slutty girls get.

I hung up the phone and lay there, imagining the way the disease had crawled up my vagina, through my uterus, enveloping my internal organs and infecting my entire body. I wondered if I should call in sick from work.

Before I freaked out, though, I called Jason, my sort-of boyfriend, who lived in Providence. We'd met in college, gone different ways, and then reconnected after we both ended serious relationships, banding together over our commiserated heartbreak. He was a lifesaver. He lived across the country, but we were talking, texting, or Skyping every day, and had become so close that I'd flown across the country to see him. He was definitely somebody who needed to know that I had chlamydia. I figured that the chances were that he'd given it to me, and I was terrified that this harsh reality would ruin our perfect whirlwind romance.

He picked up the phone after a single ring. "Morning, beautiful."

"Is this a good time to talk?"

He could clearly hear the concern in my voice. "What's up?"

I dropped the chlamydia bomb and, as expected, he was devastated. Like me, he knew very little about the disease except that it was an STD and STDs were gross.

"I can't believe this," he said.

"Me neither."

"How did this happen?"

"I guess we weren't safe." I could feel the tears well up in my eyes and I wanted nothing more than to rest my cheek on his barrel chest and feel his strong arms wrapped around me. I wanted to snuggle up against him, just like I had that weekend we'd spent together. I envisioned our mutual STD bringing us closer.

"I can't believe this," he repeated.

"I know." I found solace in the fact that we were in this mess together.

Then he said, "My girlfriend's been cheating on me."

This news slapped me in the face.

"You have a girlfriend?"

"Off and on," he said.

"For how long?"

"It was probably that ex-boyfriend she keeps hanging out with."

Just the day before, Jason had told me that he connected with me better than any other woman in his life—better than his ex-wife, better than any ex-girlfriend. He had said that I could be the love of his life. And this whole time, he'd had a girlfriend? And he was complaining about *her* cheating on *him*?

This is something they don't tell you about chlamydia: the symptoms aren't that bad. I didn't even know I had it. What's bad is when you tell a potential soul mate you have it and discover that *he has a girlfriend*.

After I hung up, I did what any normal adult with an Internet connection would do: I Googled the shit out of chlamydia. I expected to spiral down the dark hole of WebMD, but instead discovered that, out of all the STDs, chlamydia was one of the most common and curable—out of your system after one shot of antibiotics. I took the meds. I should have been relieved, but I couldn't sleep for two nights. I was obsessing about how I pick the wrong men, how I don't always use a condom, how I had foolishly let a guy go down on me for fifteen seconds that summer. Before this news, just forty-eight hours earlier, I had been an innocent girl, and maybe in love with a college sweetheart. Suddenly I was a tawdry vixen caught in a love triangle with some slut disease. I was the anecdotal story at the end of the after-school special.

Two days later, Jason called me at 4:30 AM. "Good news," he blurted out.

I was half-asleep and didn't know what he was talking about. "Huh?"

"My test results are back and I'm clean!"

Good news? For who? Chlamydia is like some weird kind of truth serum. Bring up the clap and see who people really are.

But I was too nice to yell at him. "Are you relieved?" I asked.

"Of course," he said. "Nobody wants chlamydia."

Nobody wants chlamydia. His insight was really profound.

I'd never in my life wished chlamydia on anyone else before. Until that moment: when I thought about how much I'd love for Jason to get a big scoop of chlamydia sprinkled with some HPV and a side of herpes.

How was this guy getting off scot-free? For him, it was a good day—*yay, no chlamydia for me! I can keep cheating and getting cheated on, whee!* But for me, I was a damaged woman—burned with the scarlet letter C. Had he, at any point, thought about my feelings? Maybe not that day, maybe not the next, but one day, I hope he gets a burning shot of chlamydia in the face.

I hung up the phone and lay in bed. I guessed I wouldn't be moving to the East Coast anytime soon. But this led me to another major question: if Jason didn't give me the clap, then who did? And the answer to that filled me with a heavy dread. The last person I'd slept with, ten months earlier, had been my ex of three years, Chris. And my nightmare just got worse.

To say the least, Chris had a jealous side. He was so paranoid about other guys that he'd invented a new kind of cheating: talk cheat. I'd meet a guy for coffee, and suddenly it was a "coffee cheat." Or I'd get a text from a childhood friend and that was a "text cheat." Chris would ask me, "If you're not doing anything wrong, then why are you acting so guilty?" Because I *felt* guilty. All the time. I was cheating on him with everyone—the clerk at 7-Eleven, who asked for exact change; my UCLA Extension teacher, who gave me notes on a script; my brother, who called to ask when I was coming up for Christmas.

Since our breakup, I'd worked closely with my hippie

therapist to target specific feelings of sexual shame. I grew up with traditional Chinese parents who didn't believe in sex before marriage, so I had some shit to deal with. But I worked on it, started hanging out with my male friends again, let a guy go down on me for fifteen seconds over the summer, and by December, I was rather proud of my healing process. I loved sex!

Then the clap happened. And the last thing I wanted to do was write to Chris, the judgiest of judgy people. We didn't speak to each other. He was no longer in my life. But we were adults and I figured he needed to know.

I wrote him a quick email: "Hey Chris, just wanted to let you know I tested positive for chlamydia. If you haven't been tested, you should."

My email was short and sweet, like a little kid's Valentine's Day card: "I choo-choo-choose for you to get STD-tested."

Three hours later, he emailed me back. Just seeing his name in my inbox made my stomach churn. Did he think I was slutting it up all over town?

He wrote: "I've been tested twice since we broke up and I'm clean. Other than this, I hope you're well. "

Other than this, I hope you're well? First of all, I was sure he didn't hope I was well. I was sure that Chris was at work, appreciating his clap-free testicles, and smugly reassuring himself, "That's what happens when you're easy." Second, "tested twice since we broke up?" What had *he* been doing?

The irony was that, in the previous ten months, I'd had sex for one day. *One day*. With Jason in Providence. I was practically a nun. Thanks a lot, Universe, for my immaculate infection.

I called my hippie therapist for an emergency session and told her that I had chlamydia. I added that I was obsessively going through my entire Rolodex of ex-lovers, wondering if I'd gotten it from that guy who went down on me for fifteen seconds that summer, or if I'd had it for years and it had been dormant until now.

She responded, "You're so lucky." Lucky. Really? Lucky is winning the lottery, or a new car, not getting the clap. I wanted to say, "You're fired, hippie! How dare you manipulate my misery into a positive situation?" But I let her continue: "You're being tested on something you specifically need to work on. The bigger the test, the bigger the healing. You can ask for small tests, but it'll only take you longer to heal."

By the end of that crazy week, I got an even bigger piece of information, something that had never even crossed my mind. My gynecologist called to tell me that the test results were a false positive.

I never had the clap. I was clean!

I wanted to email Chris and Jason and say, "Psych! False alarm! Who's the slut now?" But I didn't.

By then, I'd come to a place where I didn't care about what they thought of me. I had cried myself to sleep all week, contacted two exes, and in the end, I didn't judge myself too harshly. I *was* lucky. I was given chlamydia, and then it was taken away from me. Nothing had happened, but in a way, my whole life had changed.

That week made me realize that things will always come up to make me question myself but eventually, those things will pass. Turned out that faux chlamydia was a metaphor for all things in life. Like when my boss micromanages me, I'll think, "That's not because I'm doing something wrong. That's his issue." Or when I'm on page ninety-six of my movie script and can't imagine the ending, I'll think, "This is not because I can't finish it. I just need more time." Self-doubt, shame, and a false positive test result. They all have the same thing in common: with time, I learn that they were never true in the first place.

My Boyfriend, Jesus
Diana Spechler

I once dated a guy who thought he was Jesus. I don't mean he thought he was Jesus in the enlightened, we-are-all-one sense, in which case he would have thought he was also Buzz Aldrin, Bill Clinton, Hillary Clinton, and flowers. He thought he was *just* Jesus.

Granted, Jesus's delusion (let's call him Jesus; he would want it that way) reflects less poorly on him than it does on me. Why, you might ask, would I date a guy who thought he was Jesus, when there are so many guys out there who, you know, don't think they're Jesus? Especially considering the fact that I'm Jewish?

But I was twenty years old. Although being twenty isn't the same thing as having a frontal lobotomy, it is similar. And Jesus was super hot. He had blue eyes and biceps. A piano-key smile. He looked like a jock, but he'd been born and raised in Boulder, Colorado, where we were college students, so he wasn't a jock so much as the son of a yoga instructor.

Before I knew that he thought he was Jesus, before I even knew that he was hot, I met Jesus at a Halloween party where he was dressed as a vampire. Boulderites take Halloween seriously. This was no slapdash vampire costume; not only was Jesus's face painted a ghoulish purple-white, not only did he sport fangs and convincing dribbles of blood on his chin, not only did he don a floor-length cape, but he had shaved his head and gotten horns surgically embedded in his scalp. At least, they looked surgically embedded. I liked him right away due to the energy he'd expended on that costume.

We chatted briefly at the party before a girl dressed as a sexy nurse overdosed in the bathroom, convulsed on the floor, and was carted off in an ambulance. (For the record, she survived, and went on to enjoy several more overdoses, and now, I see on Facebook, she's married and has breast implants, so don't you worry about her.) Because Jesus was friends with the sexy nurse, he got so upset that he needed to go home to meditate. I was disappointed. We'd been having a great conversation about his family members, to whom he referred as his "pillars." I would soon learn that, the way Jesus saw it, everyone in his life existed just to prop him up.

∾

A couple of nights after Halloween, Jesus called me and we started dating. He took me to more parties— he consistently knew the best ones—and once, out for Mexican food. We always wound up engrossed in long conversations marked by Jesus doing all the talking. Jesus had lots of theories, mostly about himself. One of his theories was that scattered throughout the world, a group of seemingly unconnected people, seven of them to be precise, shared a mission. The mission was to love. (This sounded vague to me, Jesus explained, because I couldn't possibly understand.) Jesus was one of the seven—ironic, I see in retrospect, because he loved himself deeply and exclusively. My roommate, Julie, was also one of the seven, or in the parlance of Jesus, "One of Them," as was Jesus's friend Michael and Jesus's ex-girlfriend in Atlanta. But was I? No, no, no, not me. Perhaps I had some other life mission, such as to crochet beautiful potholders.

Jesus was exhausting, but I was too young to understand the impenetrable nature of narcissism; I saw his aloofness as a challenge, and thought I could break through and fix him, and then I would have a normal, healthy relationship with my hot boyfriend who didn't have pesky quirks like pathological self-absorption.

ᡐ

One night, Jesus came over to take Julie and me to a concert—me because we were dating and Julie because she was One of Them. Before he arrived, I asked Julie, "Do you think Jesus is crazy?" I was sitting on the rim of the bathtub, watching her blow-dry her hair.

"I think he's schizophrenic," Julie said.

We were psychology majors. We liked to diagnose our peers. But we saw unmedicated schizophrenia not as grounds for reconsidering a romantic partner, merely as a means of gossiping with nuance.

"Schizophrenic," I said, nodding. "That makes sense."

"But he's really hot," Julie conceded, finding my eyes in the mirror.

"I *know*," I squealed.

Jesus arrived bearing vodka, and the three of us drank it in the living room, a space furnished in part by a beanbag chair that spewed beans when sat on. Of course, Jesus didn't debase himself by occupying the beanbag. (I did.) He sat in a straight-backed chair and held forth like his predecessor at the Last Supper. Then he drained his glass and told us, "When my mother was pregnant with me, she prayed for a Christ child."

Julie and I glanced at each other, Julie snorted, and

then we both silently and swiftly vowed never to look at each other again.

"And," Jesus said, holding his arms open, "well." He shrugged.

"What?" I said.

"There's significant evidence," he said, "to suggest that her prayers were answered."

"Okay," I said.

"Okay!" said Julie. "Let's go!"

We stood and put on our coats. We looked at Jesus, who crossed his arms over his chest and frowned. He hated to be interrupted.

∾

And still I insisted on dating him.

Not long after Jesus confessed that he was Jesus, we were lying on my bed one evening, talking, by which I mean that Jesus was talking, when he farted.

I wondered if this would be our breakthrough, if this fart would bond us. Maybe Jesus would be embarrassed, an emotion I'd never seen him display, and of which I'd assumed him incapable. Then I could tell him it was all right, everyone farted sometimes, and he would see how understanding I was and feel close to me. Or maybe he would laugh. Even the original Jesus probably found humor in a good, booming fart.

I turned to look at Jesus. His face was serene. He farted again. I giggled. But I was getting a little grossed out. This was my bed, after all.

He turned to me and rolled his eyes. "This is why I don't date younger girls," he said, shaking his head.

"Huh?"

I was mostly confused by the "younger girls" part. I was twenty. Jesus was twenty-one.

"You're so immature," he said.

"How so?" I cried.

"Farting is natural," said Jesus, quoting the New Testament. "Your laughter is childish."

I'd like to say that I dumped him then. The suffragettes didn't march for nothing; a man can't just fart in a woman's bed and then accuse her of immaturity. We have rights.

But at twenty, I was undeterred by schizophrenia, flatulence, and manipulation. I think I might have apologized: "I'm sorry I laughed at your fart."

∾

Twelve years later, these conversation snippets haunt me:

"I'm sorry I laughed at your fart."

"My mother prayed for a Christ child."

"I take Ecstasy for spiritual purposes."

My Jesus never healed the sick, showed kindness to prostitutes, or fasted in the desert. In fact, a far cry from fasting: I once watched him wolf a beef chimichanga and wash it down with six Coronas. If he was a messiah, he wasn't a terribly ascetic one.

But if he really was Jesus, perhaps I was Mary Magdalene. And perhaps, as the Bible claims, Jesus cured me of "demons." After all, what's the point of dating a lunatic if not to get lunatics out of your system? I've never loved another Christ child, and I thank Jesus for that.

∾

Soon after he farted in my bed, Jesus broke up with me. It had been a good run, he said, but clearly I had "a lot to learn."

"About what?" I pressed.

But he wouldn't elaborate. Jesus preferred to spout cryptic wisdom. Only years later would his words sink in and make perfect, inarguable sense.

Sleeping with the Enemy

Samantha Dunn

There's no other way to tell you this. I just have to say it: I fell in love with a Republican.

Oh, believe me, it gets worse.

Not only is he a Republican, he's in up to his eyeballs. He called Henry Kissinger to tell him about Richard Nixon's funeral arrangements. His mother has a framed picture hanging in the house of her with Robert Dole, autographed with, "Thanks Sharon! Bob." His father was a pastor of an evangelical church whose defective television was built with only one channel, Fox News.

For someone like me—someone whose earliest memories are of a home with pictures of the pope and JFK hanging side by side on the wall, someone whose mother was known to say things like "God is not only Irish but also a Democrat," someone who comes from

a family of self-described "blue-bellied Yankees"—
falling for a Republican was like admitting I loved
Darth Vader.

How could this possibly happen, you ask?

At first it was the usual thing: sex appeal.

No, don't barf. Get that image of a bellicose, rotund
Rush Limbaugh out of your head. Banish thoughts of
the pasty Karl Rove and forget entirely that cretin from
Missouri who talked about "legitimate rape."

I first saw a picture of the man I love on an Internet
dating site. Why was I there? I'd dated the narcissistic
actor-screenwriter-dancer-musician-producer types on
the west side of Los Angeles to disastrous ends for far
too long. If the definition of "insanity" is doing the same
thing over and over again, then I was determined to get
sane. And sane looked to me like trying Match.com.

I know, I know. Don't look too hard at that last
sentence.

Anyway, I hadn't been on there for more than a
month when I opened my inbox and saw something
that raised goose bumps on my arms and created a
tingle in the pit of my stomach. It was a wink from
a guy named Jimmy. I took one look at the tattooed
arms, the flinty, Steve McQueen–like stare, the sardonic twist of his smile, and somehow I knew that he
would smell of hickory smoke and Old Spice, and that
the scruff of his five o'clock shadow would sometimes

rub a rash on my pale skin.

Good Lord this man was hotter than Georgia asphalt—to steal a line from *Wild at Heart*, a movie I would come to find that we both loved.

I yelled over my shoulder, "Mom, check this one out! I think this guy's looking for me."

Mom, out visiting from her retirement in New Mexico, ambled up to assess the candidate on the screen. One eyebrow went up.

"Yum, yum," came the verdict. Then she added, "But he's probably a Republican."

To her, that was like saying he looked like a man who beat his dog when he wasn't in prison. During the "terrible years," Mom had forsaken most major news outlets out of fear of coming across the latest pronouncements from George W. (Bad for her blood pressure, you understand.)

My response to her prediction was the usual *Ha ha ha, very funny, Mother, why do you always have to find fault with every guy in the world?* Or words to that effect.

You know already that the joke was on me. Four months later, I found myself seated at a swanky fund-raiser for the California Republican Party, deep in the red heart of Orange County. The tattooed bad boy named Jimmy was a well-established campaign manager and political consultant for the GOP. He'd even run Orrin Hatch's bid for president. Not only had I fallen in love with Darth Vader, I was now dining aboard the Death Star.

After the speech from then-governor Arnold Schwarzenegger to the five hundred or so assembled faithful, but before conservative radio talk show host Dennis Prager took the mic, I slipped outside with Jimmy so I could get a breath of fresh air and stop biting my tongue. He, meanwhile, was jonesing for a cancer stick.

Jimmy had forgotten matches, so he bummed a light from a woman puffing on her cigarette. The two had worked together on campaigns and fell into easy shop talk, but the woman's eyes narrowed as she began to dish about Schwarzenegger's chief of staff, who evidently leaned too far left to suit her.

"It's Maria's influence," she hissed. Did I imagine it or had her eyes hardened as she looked at us? "That's what happens when our Republican men hook up with liberal women."

Jimmy immediately became very interested in lighting another cigarette. I, meanwhile, smiled, said nothing, and thought that if this woman knew we drove here in my hybrid car she'd have me burned at the stake. Today Jimmy's driving in a hybrid, tomorrow he might join a labor union—all because of this writer chick he's dating. *When will it end?*

This would not be the last time Jimmy and I would

find ourselves in the minefield where love and politics meet. Mostly it was not the intolerant Republicans but my love-the-world, yoga-practicing, gluten-free progressive best friends who were apoplectic over my new romance. "*A Republican?* Are you that desperate? Don't you know what they are doing to our country?" (Funny, they were never as worried about the former heroin addicts.)

Some friends of mine even disinvited us from a dinner party when they found out what Jimmy did for a living. Too bad. Not only because they made an awesome artichoke risotto, but because they missed talking to him. They missed his encyclopedic knowledge of American history, his fervent love of wilderness and of the American park system, his wry sense of humor, his passion for great books, his punk-rockabilly past as a professional musician, his arrest record. They missed joining with me to tell him that he is actually socially liberal and fiscally just wrong, and they missed the argument over the fiscal part that always gets my blood going.

Mostly they missed knowing a man who turns out not only to be smoking hot—I'd tell you more, except the kids might read this someday—but also loyal to the people he loves, and fierce, and smart, and unique, and particular, a man whose sum total is not represented by any politician or confined within the doctrine of any political party. He drives me absolutely crazy at times, and there are things we will never, ever agree on, but being with him always makes me reconsider what I do believe, and why I believe it. It makes me look closer at all people, and not assume I know everything about them from their (stupid, dumb-ass) bumper stickers. (Okay, so I have to work on that part, maybe.)

I guess I need to mention here that I married him. Yep. We eloped. Could you imagine a wedding reception? If one of his family members had even just mentioned Ayn Rand, my mother would have broken a chair over somebody's head.

But the point is I realized that in all those years of dating that maybe I was the real narcissist. Maybe I was looking for someone exactly like me, who would reflect back to me exactly that which I wanted to see. Maybe if we all slept with an enemy, or at least took him to dinner, we'd understand more, maybe even find places of agreement. It happens. Take Jimmy's dad, the evangelical pastor, who now happens to be my father-in-law. We have even voted the same. Granted, it was for *Dancing with the Stars*, but, hey, it's a start.

The Ethical Slut

Chloe Caldwell

I read about *The Ethical Slut* by Dossie Easton and Janet W. Hardy in either *Time Out* or *New York* magazine in 2008. I ripped the piece out of the magazine and put it in my back jeans pocket to give to the man whom I loved and who was in love with me—and in love with someone else: his girlfriend.

The Ethical Slut discusses how to live an active life with multiple, concurrent sexual relationships in a fair and honest way. Discussion topics include how to deal with the practical difficulties and opportunities in finding and keeping partners, maintaining relationships with others, and strategies for personal growth. The article was a personal essay, recommending *The Ethical Slut* and explaining that it is possible, and maybe even healthier, to be in love with more than one person at the same time.

The man and I went out to dinner that night. It was July and we went to an Italian place in the West Village called the Flower Room. I had a red tank top on. He had a red T-shirt on. We sat at an outdoor table that had red roses on it. "Is this too romantic?" I asked him and he laughed. We drank glasses of red wine and I probably got a salad and he got pasta. From the apartment windows above the restaurant, "Waterloo Sunset" by the Kinks started to play. I handed him the article across the little table and he looked at me like he wanted to fuck my brains out.

Neither of us bought the book, though for three years we talked about how we were going to. Sometimes he'd bring up the article, when he was manic and stoned and excited and in love with me: "I love that article you gave me!" Like I was a fucking genius godsend or something. Or when we talked about how fucked-up our situation was, he'd run his hands up and down my torso, grab my tits or my ass, and say, "Yeah, well, I just think about that article you gave me."

He and his girlfriend had been sharing an apartment in the East Village for almost three years at that point. After I'd been with him for a year, I was officially and openly obsessed with her—dreaming of her most nights and writing about her most days. When I asked him to tell her about me, he complied. Five months later, when she was offered a job in Washington, DC, she left. He moved to another apartment, four blocks away.

One morning, the following July, he and I got into a nasty argument. I'd reached my arm down between the bed and wall looking for my underwear only to pull up someone else's. From Target. Size small. Light blue with a pink bow. He made us breakfast: spicy eggs and vegetables, which later made me shit my brains out. I remember sitting on the couch in my camouflage shorts while he cleaned up from breakfast.

"I had a date with a girl last night and I was embarrassed to tell you," he said.

"Did you even read *The Ethical Slut*?" I asked, knowing fully that he had not.

"Noooooooooo, did you?" Knowing fully that I had not.

"Noooo."

We were speaking in snotty five-year-old tones. We spoke like siblings in the back of a car on a long road trip. It was almost funny.

And here's the thing: we really loved each other. Still do. We were kindred spirits. Still are. We wrote each other love letters. On rolls of receipt paper, on typewriters overseas. We don't shut up around each other. We don't sit down. We're explosive.

But I am not here to talk about my love for him.

∾

Orgies, or whatever you want to call them—we had
them. The first one was at his apartment in the East
Village. His best friend and younger brother were there
and I brought my best friend. We did cocaine and kissed
and showered and drank rum and danced around
in headdresses. I gave his friend a blow job while he
fucked me from behind. My friend gave him a blow job.
It made us closer. We fell asleep in the predawn, completely loving each other, spent, with his cat at our feet.

The second orgy was at a hotel, involving the same
people minus his brother. We brought a piñata, dressed
in different outfits, and tape-recorded ourselves fucking
for hours.

Before I moved to the West Coast, I ordered *The
Ethical Slut*. I moved before it came in. Two months
later, my best friend drove across the country to visit
me and she brought it. When she left a few weeks later,
I read it. The book was well written, with original anec-
dotes and an inviting tone. I loved it. I thought I was
born anew. I could do anything. It kept me up at night.
I could feel myself getting smarter. I was fine. I would
never get jealous again. I could have polygamous relationships for my whole life. I was lucky. I texted him
from my bed about the new things I was learning, how
I was healed now. He couldn't wait to borrow it.

The authors define the term "slut" as "a person of any gender who has the courage to lead life according to the radical proposition that sex is nice and pleasure is good for you."

Courage. An underrated attribute. An elusive term. We all want to consider ourselves courageous.

Ethical.

When you are in a nonconventional relationship, and you love the person you are in it with, and the sex is to die for, it's easy to lose yourself. It's easy to confuse drowning with floating. I thought I was better than other people: my heart was stronger, my independence was stronger, my passion was stronger. My relationship was stronger because it could exist without codependence and without mundane domesticity. Neither of which I am good at. You dilute your thoughts and think that other people don't understand. But really, you are the one who does not understand that you are hurting yourself. Until you do.

My friend Sarah visited me in the Northwest and got really into *The Ethical Slut*. I told her to take it back to New York with her. At the time, she was in a relationship where they had rough sex and talked a lot about their fantasies. After reading the book, she admitted that she had always been turned on by the idea of her boyfriend getting head from other girls. The book made her feel like this was normal. She could do it.

I visited New York and the man came to see me. We spent two days together at a hotel. On Sunday night before he left, he reminded me that he wanted to borrow *The Ethical Slut*. He put it on the side of the motorcycle with our leftover Wild Turkey and rode away.

One of the reasons I loved him so much was that he had a heart bigger than his head. He is sincere and earnest and scarily childlike. He says things like, "My most Buddhist moments are in bed." He is writing a manuscript about every girl he has had a sexual encounter with. He remembers every detail. He loves them all. He explains he wants a little red wagon to put them all in and pull behind him. His working title is *I Don't Like to Let Go*.

"We believe it's okay to have sex with anybody you love," Easton and Hardy write, "and we believe in loving everybody."

That is pretty much the theme of his life.

I flew back to the West Coast. A few weeks passed and then one evening I saw three missed calls from him. He left me a voicemail. "Hey, I started *The Ethical Slut*, and I had to call you. You're right—it's amazing." I called him back and he read parts aloud to me and told me he wanted to get out of the relationship he was in. "I will never enter another relationship that inhibits the one between you and me," he said. "The relationship I'm in will end like all the others. You and I could still be standing." We stayed on the phone from seven at night to seven in the morning.

Of course, we had another argument, via email, a day later. Just now, I typed "The Ethical Slut" into my Gmail search engine and there were seventeen results. The first one I clicked on was an email from him saying, "You're so stuck in this traditional idea of relationships. Jesus, you're the one that gave me *The Ethical Slut*."

These things come back to haunt you. In truth, I was never stuck in the idea of traditional relationships. Until he wouldn't let me have one.

∾

Nothing changed. Nada, niente, at all. Four years. We cried a lot. We made love a lot. Last December, after we'd had yet another crash landing, I called my friend while I was crying and walking the streets of New York aimlessly. "Chloe," she said. "You guys spent three years being shady for dopamine." It's never been better said. We were cheaters, liars; we were addicted to a feeling we'd created. There was not one ethical thing about it. It was the opposite of ethical. Self-help books don't save lives. Go figure.

Our relationship ended up breaking both of our hearts. The last thing he said was: "We're a mess. We've always been a mess. But I still love you and I still think we're going to have our chance. But I'm not asking you to wait, or to do anything. I'll come find you."

The part of me that loves him saw the romance in this. Saw the romance in his someday coming to find me, his motorcycle zooming up to my apartment, where we would embrace and he would give me my book back and we would have landed. We would be home. But the part of me that wants to love myself, the part of me that cried in bars and in my mother's bed and his bed, the part of me that had to deal with my anxious desperate depression, and the part of me that couldn't let go for years—that was the part that responded:

"Don't. Don't ever."

We had our chance.

He still has the book. And frankly, I have no desire to own *The Ethical Slut,* or the man that wants to be an Ethical Slut. I don't want to be an Ethical Slut. I want to be an Ethical Person. I will say this: as much as I love the idea, as much as I think it's a wonderful book, I don't think being an Ethical Slut is possible. At least not for him. At least not for me. At least not in New York City. Maybe in San Francisco.

Fresh Step

Vanessa Marshall

It's not that I don't see red flags; it's that I am the type of person who paints them white. Yearning for connection, I can turn any suspect occurrence into a completely plausible, acceptable situation. But sometimes even I can't be fooled.

I met him when I was at Princeton. I knew he came from a wealthy, conservative family, but I didn't pay much attention to him. Years later, he found me on Facebook. He actually looked pretty good. He'd aged well. And his relationship status? Single. I wondered if after all these years, we'd finally found each other.

I agreed to see him when he visited Los Angeles from New York City. His line of work? Hedge funds. I suppose that should have been the first red flag.

He stayed at the Chateau Marmont, and he looked

even better in person. Like Antonio Banderas with a beard. We had a lovely dinner: steak frites, crème brûlée, and eventually a romantic kiss goodnight. He was a perfect gentleman.

The next day, when I went back for another visit, the warnings started. He joined me in the lobby, wearing red Gucci loafers, no socks, and plaid shorts. (Really?) Then he kissed my hand and asked, "You ready for some brekkie?"

I looked at his hairy, pale legs sticking out of those crimson loafers and asked, "Brekkie?"

"Breakfast, dahling!"

Gentlemen who may be reading this: I can assure you, if you ever want to get laid ever again, never, ever ask us if we want any "brekkie." That was probably red flag number two. Or three—if you count the shoes. Or maybe four—for no socks. Okay, five for the plaid shorts. But who's counting anymore?

So I just kept my eyes above his waist and told myself that this must be how people from Exeter and Andover talk and that it wasn't his fault how he was raised. It wasn't his choice to be born into wealth like a Rockefeller. And besides, my mother would love him.

We walked over to Book Soup so he could get some magazines. I got *Sports Illustrated, Details,* and *Esquire.* He got *Vogue, Glamour,* and *Cosmo* "for the articles." I officially stopped counting red flags then.

Most women would have said goodbye at that point, but I told myself, "Here is a man so curious about women that he dares to read up on their fashion. He cares. He's progressive. Ballsy. I like it."

We returned to the Chateau and enjoyed drinks by the pool. Thumbing through the *Cosmo* article—"He Started Eating Rice with His Hands and Other WTF Date Stories"—he began to tell me more about his work. "I'm looking for investors for a new company," he said. "It's very exciting. They're going to drill for oil."

"Really? Where?"

"Off the shore of Alaska."

"Near the Arctic National Wildlife Refuge?" I wasn't sure I really wanted to hear the answer.

"Yes, right off ANWR," he answered. Before I could roll my eyes, he grabbed his Prada man purse and produced maps with thermographic images. There were charts with color-coded speculations. This all seemed a bit much for a casual conversation.

"Is that a brochure?"

"Yes, as a matter of fact, it is."

"For me?"

"You can have it," he said, handing it to me.

"No, I'm good."

"Take it!"

"No, really. I'm good," I said, handing it back to

him a bit forcefully. "I have no interest in drilling near the home of the Porcupine caribou."

"It would actually be an excellent investment for you, Vanessa. They will be producing a million barrels of oil a day."

"Seriously," I said, "it's not for me. Images of the *Exxon Valdez* oil spill still haunt me. I couldn't possibly."

"But we have such limited resources in this country."

"*I* have such limited resources!" I said jokingly, hoping he would stop pitching his crap idea to me.

"How big is your stock portfolio?"

I was speechless. "How big is your penis?" I wanted to ask. Equally inappropriate. But I couldn't speak.

"You would only need to invest $25,000," he continued.

"I don't really—"

"How big is your portfolio?"

Again I was silent.

"You should really know these things," he advised.

"I do know these things," I said defensively. "And I know my stockbroker would never go for this."

"Look, Vanessa, your stockbroker is your employee. All you have to do is ring him up and simply tell him to cash out some stocks."

To shut this guy up, I finally said, "Let me think about it." He winked, exhaled, and put his maps away.

At this point, I was clearly looking at a red flag parade. Did he come here to woo me or to sheist me out of $25,000? Again, most women would have fled the scene for political reasons alone. I was indeed skeptical and very hesitant, but I told myself that he must really believe all his little charts, and perhaps he thinks he's actually doing me a favor by getting me in on the ground floor. Maybe he landed on the topic entirely by accident? He was just making conversation, and then it organically evolved into a full-blown presentation.

Then I wondered if we could be the next great bipartisan couple. Like James Carville and Mary Matalin, we could grudge fuck every night. I could try to screw the ignorance out of him. I do like a challenge. Plus, our kiss the night before had been good. I decided I needed to investigate further.

He wanted to see where I lived, so we went back to my place. He loved it. Good sign. It was lunchtime by then and I had nothing to offer him in the way of food so I ran out to get some snacks. He told me to hurry back.

And I did, with sushi, fresh fruit, and a newly opened mind. During my errand, I'd reminded myself that trusting what I thought were my instincts when it came to romance had gotten me in trouble in the past and that I was never going to date a new type of person if I was going to be so judgmental. But when I returned, he had a dark look on his face.

"Vanessa, I need to tell you something," he began.

He was so visibly upset I wasn't sure if he was going to come out to me or confess that he'd been molested.

He began, "I . . . I had an upset stomach."

"Okay."

"Downstairs."

"Okay."

"I had to go. Number two."

"So what's your point?"

"I wanted you to know that I used the toilet downstairs. And I think it is broken."

"Oh yeah. I shut the water off on that toilet because it was running. You took a crap in there?"

"Well, sort of . . ."

"I am not following you here."

"I made a mess," he said, tears now in his eyes.

"That activity is rarely clean."

"I know but . . . it wouldn't go down the toilet."

"Meaning?"

"I used the cat box."

"What?"

"I used the litter box. Beside the toilet."

"Wait, are you saying that you lifted shit out of the bowl and put it in the box?"

"In a manner of speaking."

"Or in a manner of speaking, did you shit in my cat box?"

"...Yes."

Nothing can prepare you for a moment like this.

He said, "But I removed the offending material."

"Um, where did you put it?"

"Outside. In the trash."

Now it's one thing to shit in a cat box but it's quite another thing to *tell* someone about it. *Why wouldn't you just act like nothing happened?* Who had to know? Why would you ever tell someone, especially someone with whom you hoped to have relations—sexual or otherwise?

I asked him to stop talking. I drove him to LAX in silence. I never saw him again.

Did he actually think that I'd assume my cat took the biggest shit of her life? Was that his initial line of reasoning, but when he saw his turd in the litter, he realized how impossible it would be for a small animal to create it?

So please allow me to say to any gentlemen who may be reading this: if you ever, ever want to get laid, ever again, never, ever shit in the cat box.

Because that's an undeniable red flag.

Love—or
Something Like It

The Tantra

Rachel Shukert

I've heard that one-night stands are supposed to make women feel cheap and unwanted. Women, it is supposed, are so desperate for validation, so starved for love and attention, that a sexual encounter not shortly thereafter followed by a halting phone message or awkward meal must denote a lapse in judgment so blatant and reprehensible that the simple act of getting home is dubbed the "walk of shame," a Via Dolorosa for the urban would-be Magdalene, existing under the premise that there is nothing more embarrassing in the world than receiving a knowing wink from the deli guy.

I, however, have rarely felt less ashamed than when limping down the subway steps in too-high heels with a crushing hangover and mascara smeared down my cheeks. On the contrary. For me, casual sex brought with it a triumphant feeling, one of hope and possibility, bringing me time and time again from the precipice of panic and self-loathing in a way the makers of Zoloft could only dream of. Pointless, self-involved, slightly dangerous sex. It was one of those things, like Scrabble, pizza, and irony, that made life worth living.

Then I got married.

If sex was to be the antidote to many woes, it now had to be married sex. *Meaningful* sex. *Wholesome* sex.

Gross.

∾

The CAP21 studios on West Eighteenth Street, where the musical theater stars of tomorrow are designed, assembled, and trained, were abuzz with activity. Some sort of audition process was afoot, and the lobby was clogged with nervous girls with fake Louis Vuitton bags and the graceful, gay boys that pretend to love them clutching the real ones, all of them chatting cattily about classmates while engaged in some seriously competitive stretching.

"She has, like, no head voice at all," said one girl, running a brush through her carefully highlighted hair, with legs in the splits.

"She's got brassy tone—brassy, brassy, brassy," said her elfin companion, pausing to adjust the bulge in his dance belt before bringing his nose to rest against his knees.

I attended NYU drama myself, albeit in a more "experimental" capacity, which means that it often involved watching a classmate perform a postmodern movement piece involving gravel or nudity or bacon. Still, I felt more than a twinge of envy toward the plucky little triple-threats over at CAP21, with their jazz shoes and their headshots and their alarming range of movement. So I was excited just to be here in the thick of it all.

So excited that I was very startled when a woman with a clipboard approached my husband and me.

"Umm . . . are you here for the tantric sex workshop?" she asked quietly.

"Yes," Ben said, giving me a look that said, *It's not too late to run.* "We are."

The clipboard woman led us down a long corridor lined with bulletin boards full of headshots and casting notices. Passing an open studio door, we heard the first lugubrious strains of "The Music of the Night" from *The Phantom of the Opera* springing from the throat of a lithe pixie of a boy, each eyebrow, plucked to a perfect circumflex, straining beneath his shining forehead.

"You're sure we don't have to get naked?" Ben whispered.

"I'm sure."

"Do we have to see anyone else naked?"

"I hope so."

We entered a smallish, slightly shabby studio at the very end of the hallway, where other couples were already assembled. We had been instructed to wear comfortable, loose-fitting clothing, and it was a strange feeling to be in a room full of strangers wearing their pajamas. Our instructor, Shelley, was standing in the middle of the room, smiling warmly. She appeared to be in her mid- to late forties, and was very thin, with longish, lank hair and a large chin and mouth that made her look kind of like Janice from the Muppets. I don't mean this as an insult.

On the other side of the room, beside a makeshift altar littered with scarves and little Buddhas and other detritus of enlightenment, was a man staring at our instructor with a look of studied, focused benignity. He wore an embroidered blouse and soft, zipperless pants—the kind a baby might wear.

"This is Walter," Shelley said, "my partner."

Ben and I had assumed we'd be the youngest couple there, but everyone seemed to be about our age. We settled on the floor next to another couple, a pink-haired girl wearing a Misfits T-shirt and her preppy boyfriend.

"Hi!" I said, cheerfully.

They smiled back, tentatively, like I was being really, really friendly in the bathroom.

"We don't have to get naked, right?" Ben whispered to me, for the fourth time. He hugged his bare knees to his chest.

"I'm very happy to see you all," Shelley continued in a slow, calm voice. "Let me tell you a little bit about myself. I'm originally from Pittsburgh. I began studying this discipline in India about . . . well, a long time ago, and I've been teaching these workshops now for about nineteen years. My partner, Walter, is newer to the discipline, but he's still very excited to share his experience and knowledge with you."

Walter said nothing. He stared directly at Shelley with an expression that, it occurred to me, was not so much beatific as his idea of beatific.

"Rachel!" Ben hissed.

"What?"

Shelley was staring at me, with serene annoyance. "We were just going around the circle and introducing ourselves."

I hissed at Ben. "Why couldn't you do it?"

"This is your thing, remember?" he shot back.

We were fighting at our sex lesson.

"Hi!" I exclaimed brightly. "My name is Rachel and this is Ben. And we just got married!"

A collective "aww" went up from the assembled lovers.

"How long have you been together?" Shelley asked.

"About two years."

"And what are you hoping to achieve here? Let's hear from Ben."

"Well," he began. "I guess I'm . . . just looking for some ways to feel closer and more aware of each other . . ."

This happens when Ben speaks. Just a few syllables of his plummy tones and a hush settles over the room.

"Do I detect a bit of an accent?" asked Shelley, girlishly. "Are you English?"

"South African."

"I've heard it's so beautiful there," said Shelley. "Wow. What a . . . *dynamic* place that must be."

Not only had we fought in front of the sex teacher, now the sex teacher was coming on to my husband.

We moved on, around the circle, meeting our fellow travelers. The pink-haired girl, Kelly, had been with her computer programmer beau, Steven, for seven years, and he'd had no idea of her plan for them to spend the next two hours engrossed in a world of genital mysticism until that very evening. Next we learned that Scott and his much younger girlfriend, Karen, who were neatly outfitted in coordinating track suits over pale turtlenecks, had been together just three months and were the honeymooners of the group; Mohan and Jeanine, both in their early twenties, had been together ten months. All the couples were fiercely, almost competitively, affectionate with each other. Not to be outdone, I cuddled close to Ben and wedged my head in the hollow of his neck, kissing the little tuft of hair that peeked out from the top of his T-shirt.

"Stop it," he hissed.

Everyone was hoping for increased intimacy, closeness, and a deeper spiritual connection with their partner. I noticed that no one mentioned the practical reason that we were there—to have hotter sex.

But we weren't going to do that in class, not with the pictures of Jerome Robbins on the walls. What we were going to do, after touching our toes a few times and taking some long, grounding breaths, was sit opposite each other on the floor, gazing deeply into one another's eyes. When we felt ready, we would place our hands in our partner's hands and breathe together, in unison, taking in everything about our partner. We would run our fingers over our partner's face while lovingly describing his nose, ears, and chin. Then we would take his hands again in our own, press them to our hearts, and tell him the precise reason why we loved him so much.

Well, first we were going to watch Shelley and Walter do it.

Shelley reached behind her back to turn on a small tape deck, which began to play Maria Callas singing, "O Mio Babbino Caro."

I love opera for the same reason I love figure

skating; I find it profoundly moving to watch
someone do something that hard, for no comprehen-
sible purpose other than bewildering beauty. I hear
those notes emerging from a human throat, the utter
totality of human emotion, the whole thing a testament to the unabashed silliness of human existence,
and think—*the ridiculous things we spend countless
hours learning! The laughable gravitas with which we
treat each other's fickle hearts! The absurd, irrational,
glorious mayhem of the world!*—and the tears start to
fall, thick and fast, as I think about how beautiful and
sad it is to be alive, and sometimes, yes sometimes, I
go and admire myself and my sensitivity in the mirror.
Yes, I look in the mirror when I cry. Shut up. I bet you
do it, too.

Maria Callas hit the first high A of the aria, strong
and clear, as Walter reached over and stroked Shelley's
face. Her eyes were wet. I snuggled close to Ben.

"Is your lingam hard?" I whispered.

"Not even close," he replied.

The music changed to the famous theme from *Swan
Lake*. Shelley placed Walter's hand against her heart
and began to speak, as I pictured all the little enchanted
swans fluttering around her—cursed, sad, and thin.

"I love you because . . . well . . . I wanted to talk about
that time a couple of weeks ago, when I was going through
all that stuff with Brian and the deed to the house . . ."

Now this was interesting. Who was Brian, and what was he doing with the deed to Shelley's house?

"And he was making all those sort of . . . I don't know . . . threats, and I was wondering all those things about my life, if he was right about the things that he was saying, and I was just kind of a mess . . ."

"Yes," said Walter.

"And you just held me, and I could feel your entire essence wrapped around me, like a wonderful warm blanket, and I laid my head on your chest and I just"— here she looked up at the ceiling with a prayerful smile, like a character on a soap opera—"I cried. On your chest, like I was a little girl. And I felt so loved, and so safe, and like everything was going to be all right, with this incredible support and this incredible presence that you were giving me. You were just so present and I felt so loved."

Is one's presence measured by how infrequently one blinks? Because if that's the case, then Walter was so present that he lived inside each one of us, like God.

Now it was our turn. When Ben and I turned to face each other on the floor, I burst out laughing.

My husband often tells me that I don't seem to live in the present. I'm always either a step ahead or a step behind—reminiscing, analyzing, planning, worrying. He says I don't so much have an inner life as simply a life that is sometimes, though seldomly, forced to interact with the outside world.

And he's right. I don't live in the present. I interview myself in my head when I walk down the street. I live in either an imaginary past of faded glory or a future filled with promises of it. And when I am supposed to tell Ben what I love about him, I can't think of a single thing.

"I love you because . . . I don't know. Because I love you."

"And?"

"You're nice . . . to me. Sometimes. You're very supportive."

"I'm . . . supportive?"

"Yes! And you're . . . handsome?"

"Okay."

"And funny!"

"Okay."

"And I just love you, okay? Why can't I just love you because I love you?"

"You can. It's fine."

"No! I have to think of something, or I'm a terrible person."

"Rachel," Ben said. "Don't worry about it." He pressed my hand emphatically and leaned in close. *"This is kind of stupid."*

"Okay, everybody," Shelley beamed, wiping tears from her eyes. "Now what we're going to do is a sort of sexual breathing exercise. The Shiva is going to take a deep breath from his heart, and let that breath travel down to his genitals, then breathe it out into the yoni of the goddess. Then, goddesses, let the breath travel up through your heart, and breathe it out again to your Shiva."

Okay. So Ben was supposed to suck up a nice big gulp of air through his urethra, visualize it traveling magically to his open heart, where it would be expelled in a puff of fairy dust into my chest, where I would catch it, cradle it for a moment, and then push back out from my vagina?

"Watch out," I whispered. "I'm sending you the sparkliest queef you ever saw."

He grinned. I grinned back. I never feel so close to my husband as when we are united in scorn for something we know next to nothing about. We have our own manner of loving, Ben and I. It expresses itself in mockery and pejorative nicknames, in depantsing and brief, playful sex. It cannot be taught; not by tantric goddesses nor men in blouses. We may be terrible people, but at least we have each other.

To Love, to Cherish, to Watch HBO

Meghan Daum

*B*ack in the fall of 2011, my husband and I spent nearly every moment of our nonworking time watching *The Sopranos* on DVD. Neither of us had caught the series the first time around. It aired between 1999 and 2007, years when my husband was working as a journalist in far-flung corners of the world and I (how's this for an exotic excuse?) was too broke to afford cable. But one day, as though finally deciding to really dig into Shakespeare, we thought it was about time we got around to it. We watched about four times a week, usually one but quite often two episodes per sitting. Before we took up with *The Sopranos* we'd watched *Breaking Bad* and *Mad Men*, in each case first on DVD and then as they aired on television. Before that we'd watched all five seasons of *The Wire* in about a three-month period. Along the way we even got stuck on a noncable series, the brilliant *Friday Night Lights*, about which we evangelized to anyone who hadn't seen it and whose series finale had us both in tears.

Now that it's 2013 and the concept of "binge watching" has become so universal that Netflix is actually creating shows to be viewed in giant, gluttonous gulps, we are doing our part and inhaling *House of Cards* and *Orange Is the New Black*. But that's only until the second half of season five of *Breaking Bad* comes along later in the summer and *Homeland* returns in the fall.

Over the years with these programs, we've both regularly had dreams about various storylines and found ourselves talking about the characters as though they were people we knew in real life. During the *Sopranos* era, apropos of nothing, my husband yelled to me from the shower, "I can't believe he's just going around like nothing happened!" I knew immediately he was talking about the *Sopranos* character Christopher Moltisanti and the recent "whacking" of his fiancée, who'd been talking to the Feds. So ingrained into our daily imaginative lives have these people become, so much more vivid are their circumstances and narratives than those of most people we actually know, we scarcely need to refer to them by their names.

My husband and I have been married for nearly four years and lived together for nearly three years before that. The ritualized television watching began six months or so after we met, when the fervent dinners in dark Indian restaurants that signify new romance began to give way to more quotidian pastimes, namely eating dinner in front of the television at one or the other's house. Today, we have our own house with a proper dining room, but several times a week (which is to say every night we're home for dinner) we carry our plates into the den, fire up the DVR or DVD player, and settle in for an hour or more of whatever series currently has us in its thrall. Before we braved the frontier of streaming, my role as the official orderer and returner of Netflix discs required such an acute awareness of how many nights' worth of viewing were on hand that I was not unlike an alcoholic keeping track of her stash. When a disc froze up or pixilated into inoperability (not so rare on those well-traveled *Sopranos* DVDs), my husband and I were not above letting out a string of expletives more appropriate for the occasion of the car not starting when you're late for work. You'd think the heart had been ripped from our entire day. And you'd be right.

You may by now have gotten the impression that we are—not to put too fine a point on it—complete losers. At the very least, you are assuming that this is the point in the discussion wherein I issue a cry for help. Trendy as binge watching may have become, this slack-jawed devotion to TV, this mindless chewing of our cud while training our eyes on a flat-screened, high-def horizon, is surely a sign of the apocalypse. At the very least, it would seem not to bode well for our marriage. As (relative) newlyweds we should be talking walks in the neighborhood, giddily cooking Mario Batali meals together, reading Tolstoy aloud to each other in bed. Instead of watching TV four nights a week and talking about it seven nights a week, we should be seeing friends, discussing our work, raising children, or at least playing with the dog. The thing is, though, minus the kids (and, admittedly, the Batali and the Tolstoy), we do most of those things. The nights that we are not watching television we are out to dinner, at parties or concerts, or attending readings. We can easily throw a barbecue and pack in seventy-five people. We play with and talk to and walk the dog incessantly. We may not feel at every minute like one of Tolstoy's "happy families" (we argue, we run out of margarine, we wonder what the hell we're doing with our lives), but nor are we anything close to unhappy or lonely or unfulfilled. We always have something to talk about. And part of the reason for that, I would argue, is that when we run out of things to say to each other, we can always talk about what we're watching on TV. In that sense, high-end television drama helps keep our relationship afloat. And I suspect we're not the only ones.

Is it any coincidence that the divorce rate in the U.S. and Britain started going down in the early to mid aughts, right around the time *The Sopranos* became a major cultural force and HBO became a powerhouse of unprecedentedly intelligent and addictive dramatic programming? Well, it might be. For all the studies on the effects of television on children, there's been little if any scientific research on the relationship between TV watching and relationships themselves, particularly committed, cohabitating partnerships. But, anecdotally speaking, I've noticed over the years that even some of the most troubled couples (ones for whom the problem of running out of margarine is dwarfed by the problem of wanting to permanently run out the door) have been able to come together over *Mad Men* or *True Blood* or *Six Feet Under,* or even the recent remake of *Battlestar Galactica* (hard as we tried, we couldn't get into that one). It isn't just that serial philanderers and vengeful vampires have a way of putting the less appealing qualities of our own partners into perspective. It isn't even the way these shows allow couples to sit for an hour (or, in our case when we were watching *The Wire,* sometimes up to five hours straight) without looking at or necessarily speaking to each other. The way I see it, what makes these shows such (as a therapist might say) *vehicles of intimacy* is the way they let us work out our own interpersonal conflicts and moral dilemmas via the safe channels provided by their characters. They let us talk about Tony and Carmela rather than our in-laws. They allow the loaded cannon of full-time mom misery to be shot off via Don and Betty Draper rather than via something much closer to home. They give us something to whisper about at night, a pillow talk that lets us work out our own problems while pretending to be gossiping about someone else's. After watching the final episode of *Six Feet Under*, which concluded with one character's premonitions of how every other character would die, my husband and I sat on the couch and sobbed for half an hour. I could be wrong, but I suspect this might have had more to do with our own families than with the Fisher family. Best of all, we avoided the subject of our own families altogether.

You could make the argument that a certain slave-like devotion to entertainment was always thus. Since the advent of radio in the 1920s, serialized storytelling has been an intrinsic part of what it means to spend an evening at home. From 1930s radio dramas like *The Shadow* to 1980s primetime soaps like *Dallas*, couples (and, by extension, families) have always been able to take the edge off the daily emotional grind by engaging in heady debates about Orson Welles's performance or, more prosaically, who shot J.R. But I'm not the first to point out that at no other time in history has such a high level of storytelling made its way into average households on such a consistent basis. Shows like *Dallas* might have had big ratings and functioned as cultural touchstones, but one needn't be a seasoned television critic to see the ways in which *The Sopranos* made *Dallas* or even the revolutionary-in-its-time if hopelessly self-conscious *Thirtysomething* look a bit like parodies of themselves.

Still, as good as these shows are, I don't think our enmeshment is entirely a matter of brilliant character arcs and virtuosic plot structure. I think it might have something to do with the changing contours of real-life arcs and structures. Television might live in two dimensions (unless you've bought one of those 3-D television sets) but so too do a lot of human beings these days. For all the aforementioned barbecues and dinner parties, my husband and I encounter far more of our friends via the mad pastiche of Facebook updates or the shrieking chorus of Twitter, where they exuberantly share their most recent doings, often via snapshots captured by mobile phone—"Sophie's first day at school!" "lentil soup for lunch!" "weird mole on chin!"—with us and the hundreds of others they've deemed worthy of such intimacies. In many cases, such as with old grammar school friends, we know nothing of the broad strokes of their lives. We have no idea where they went to college, who they married, whether their parents are still living. Yet we receive regular updates about their

workout regimes or their puppy's housetraining progress. We know nothing, in other words, about the stuff
that's made them who they are, that motivates their
actions, that comprises (as a screenwriter might say)
the "beats" of their story.

But we know Tony Soprano. And Don Draper and
Sookie Stackhouse and all those people from *The Wire*
who we can't help calling by their *Wire* names when
the actors show up on different shows playing entirely
different characters. We know them in the important
ways (what they say in therapy, how they're living a
double life, whether they're capable of murder) rather
than the lentil soup ways. And in an intimate relationship, those are the ways that matter. These big dramas,
like committed partnerships, are marathons as opposed
to sprints. The action tends to unfold over years, even
decades; people separate and reunite, divorce and
remarry, grow up, grow old, and die. To sit on the
couch with our beloved every night and watch these
epics is to be forced to recognize that much of this
will happen to us as well. Maybe not in such dramatic
fashion but certainly in some fashion. And as unsettling
as that is, it makes running out of margarine or wondering what the hell we're doing with our lives seem
less important. Or, at the very least, less interesting.

Summer Camp

Jillian Lauren

I went to sleepaway camp in upstate New York every year starting when I was eight years old. The camp I went to was a scandal—kind of like the movie *Meatballs*. We weren't so great at baseball, but we were pros at summer romances. I was twelve years old and dumping Sun-In in my hair and tanning with baby oil and newly shaving my legs when I had my first real boyfriend. His name was Greg and we never did more than kiss dryly with closed lips. And I was willing to do more but I didn't know how and anyway it seemed like it should have been up to Greg to try. One day, as we were riding in a paddleboat on the lake, Greg asked, "Are you a prude?"

And I responded, "No!" Even though I had no idea what that was. But it was clear just from the sound of it that this was something you did *not* want to be. He broke up with me that night anyway. And when I asked my girlfriends later what a prude was, I was so embarrassed. And I thought, *You little pussy, you didn't even try*. I felt for the first time the sting of rejection—and, man, did it suck. It doubled me over.

But I got up the next morning and made a big show of being just fine and I told myself that I *was* just fine, because I had a secret crush that no one knew about. My secret crush all summer—through every dry kiss with that freckly, skinny weasel Greg—had been the archery counselor, Nathan. Nathan was tall and slouchy and had more style than that camp full of spoiled Jewish kids from Long Island had ever seen. He wore his shorts low on his hips with his boxers peeking out the top and he had dyed blond hair that fell over one eye. Best of all, he was from New York City. Like with all too-cool people, there were all kinds of rumors about Nathan. He was supposedly bisexual. And friends with Morrissey. He was a model for the United Colors of Benetton. My crush on him felt more like my crush on John Travolta than my crush on Greg. Not so much because I was twelve and he was twenty-one and it was illegal as because he seemed too glamorous to ever be attainable.

But one day at archery, when Nathan stood behind me to correct my stance, an electrical charge passed between us that was unlike anything I'd ever felt before. My whole chest seemed to tighten around it.

And after that, I decided that I was going to learn to really shoot an arrow. So every day I started going to archery. It never occurred to me that I might be being obvious. Until one unusually chilly evening, when he looked at my pink, fuzzy Benetton sweater with a white *B* on it and knowingly said, "Benetton." Then he reached into his pocket and gave me a Benetton pin. He had a Benetton pin in his *pocket*. It was a Benetton cosmic sign. I put it like a talisman on a shelf over my head; I took it down and looked at it 2,700 times a day. I ran my fingers along the edges of it and studied it for secret messages.

And it went on like this for weeks, until one night I set my alarm for 3:00 AM and hid it under my pillow. It wasn't totally unheard of to sneak over to the boys' side of camp in the middle of the night. It wasn't allowed, of course, but we still did it sometimes: small groups of giggling girls who never really did anything once we got there.

But that night, it was different. I walked out the door alone, and began a long, scary walk in the dark, through fields of cows and skunks and probably Jason from *Friday the 13th*. I was absolutely trembling with terror. I sang Billy Joel to myself as I walked. "Brenda and Eddie were the popular steadies. And the king and the queen of the prom. Riding around with the car top down and the radio on . . ."

Finally I reached his bunk, where he was the counselor of the eight-year-old boys. It smelled like feet and mold and there were clothes strewn around on the floor. I was extra careful not to wake anyone. If I were to be caught, it would be very, very bad.

I found his bed and wondered, *What if he sends me away? What if he doesn't? What will I do then?* I didn't even know exactly why I was there. I only knew that my feelings for Nathan were so overwhelming, it was like my chest was going to cave in. There had to be some way to relieve this suffering. I wasn't sure what it was, but I knew it wasn't going to happen by the light of day.

I reached out and touched his bare shoulder to wake him. He opened his eyes and saw me and didn't seem surprised at all. He sat up and patted the bed next to him. I sat down.

"Are you alone?" he asked.

"Yeah."

"Give me your gum."

He held out his hand and I spit my gum into it. He stuck it on the windowsill and then cupped my face in his hands and leaned in to kiss me. To *French* kiss me. I thought that this was my first real kiss and maybe I'd want to remember it someday. And I was thinking, *That was so easy.*

He leaned down again and kissed my neck and I felt like I was in some great movie and then he swirled his tongue around in my ear and I thought it was disgusting (I still think it's disgusting). I wondered if that meant he was a pervert.

Then he suggested we go stand out on the porch, so we didn't wake anyone. He was much taller than me. He leaned on the porch railing with his legs apart and me standing between them and we made out like that.

He whispered in my ear, "Do you even know how I feel when I have to look at you every day running around in your shorts and you're so pretty and I can't even tell anyone?"

I didn't know what to say.

His hands moved around from my back to my still-braless bee-sting breasts and I got that feeling I had when a friend's older sister taught me to inhale the smoke from her Virginia Slims cigarette the summer before: kind of dizzy and nauseated and wondering if I had taken some kind of irreversible step, had crossed some invisible line from which there was no return.

In retrospect, I don't think smoking the Virginia Slim crossed any such line. But I do think it was crossed that night on the porch.

Over the next couple of weeks, I went to see him every night until I was exhausted and confused and in way over my head. I wanted it to stop and I wanted it never to stop and I didn't know what to do. But eventually we were caught and there was a horrifying tribunal in which I was called on the carpet and forced to testify against him and I refused and lied and was berated and humiliated by the staff and they fired him anyway. I never saw him again.

I read a letter that he wrote to my counselor before he left, and in it he said, "Please take care of her and tell her I love her and that they can't keep me from her forever." And that very thought would be the source of both my fantasies and my nightmares for years to come.

My Lesbian Love Letter from Prison

Jill Morley

*F*an letters come in spurts. When you act in a play or a film or write a widely publicized story, they come in bunches—usually. But sometimes there are strays. Not like I get a whole lot of them, mind you, but when you put your stuff out into the world, people are bound to respond . . . from all walks of life.

A few years ago I wrote an article for a national magazine based on a documentary film I'd made about working as a stripper. This generated interest from VH1, an interview on a popular New York radio station, phone calls, letters from long-lost friends, and a few "fan" letters. One of them I received a year after my article was published. My "fan," Catalin, who wrote in girly red cursive, asked me to excuse the delay in responding to the article but told me to look at the address, which would explain why she was out of the loop. She was incarcerated—in a federal prison in Pennsylvania. It was an eight-page handwritten letter mostly ranting about the prison system and how our country was becoming a police state full of "rats, snitches, and stool pigeons"—you know, normal stuff. Normal for an inmate who had the time to write such a letter. Literally a lifetime.

I have been a magnet for these people. I've dabbled in several underground worlds besides stripping—including undercover work, nightclub life, fetish videos, and training as a boxer/martial artist—and they can smell it on me. Very extreme people have crossed my path and, for a long time, I would get involved with them to an unhealthy degree. Some people called it an addiction to danger. I just thought it kept life interesting. I never understood why I shouldn't get involved with a guy who was an alcoholic, or a player, or just a plain old loser. At least I had fascinating stories to tell.

After about three pages of ranting, Catalin asked me to consider writing about the prison system inequities. Then she said that if I didn't like that idea, she had another one. She pitched me a feature film involving an average Joe who couldn't keep a job and had a miserable love life. Things just didn't seem to happen for him. While sitting in a topless bar, Joe has an epiphany: he decides to work as a female stripper. He gets breast implants, waxes his body, and gets himself a luxurious wig. Joe becomes wildly successful, makes tons of money, and gives blow jobs for $300 to $500 a pop.

The blow job prices made me think that this was coming from personal experience. Perhaps Catalin was a high-class hooker who got busted one night because she didn't suss out the undercover cop who came in for a BJ. She probably gave him one before he busted her. I think that because I watch *Law and Order* obsessively, I can make assumptions like this.

So one night Joe gets drunk and high and decides to take off his G-string while performing. His tape comes undone, his "thingie" comes out, and he urinates on the stage and the audience. Due to the closed-circuit lighting on the stage, he is fatally electrocuted. This scene, according to Catalin, should be scored by Madonna's "Like a Virgin."

Most definitely.

Catalin went on to compliment me on my article and the pictures of me that she'd seen before apologizing for not being able to see or read any of my other work in the last few years or to take me out and promise me "undying love." She told me I had "a nice (ass) smile." She drew a smiley face as if it were an email . . . but it wasn't. It was a handwritten letter from a federal prison. The letter went on to say:

*But please don't let my sense of humor or lack
thereof scare you. I am completely harmless (am
I?). Yes ma'am, especially now (frown face).
Although I could have typed this letter, I chose
to handwrite it so you could take it to a writing
analyst and find out whether or not I am some
type of psychopath (smiley face). I assure you I
am not, but just in case don't trust the analyst
either . . . my sense of humor again . . . partly
responsible for why I'm here.*

∾

Poor thing. Jailed for having a dark sense of humor.
That could easily be me. I wondered why she overused
the Smiley Face thing but figured she was in prison and
it probably made her happy to see a smile, even if it was
just a flat one drawn on paper.

The letter ended with:

*Take care and enjoy life. Be kind to others. Trust
no one. (One or two exceptions allowed.) Love
animals, children, and the elderly because they
are cute, innocent, and harmless.*
                              Best Wishes,
                              Catalin

PS Please write back.

She wrote her inmate number neatly beneath her name.

Awww. My first lesbian love letter from an inmate. I was honored. And excited. Having never been to prison before, I found it intriguing and kind of sexy. This was untapped danger territory for me. Criminals who were actually imprisoned had been tough for me to get to before this.

Yes, I had been working on getting myself back "into the light" as far as my interests go. Having lost two friends to their overexplorations into dark territories, I'd been looking to find the joy in life aboveground.

But, ever since seeing *Chicago*, I'd found the idea of women in prison glamorous. I pictured Catalin in a glimmery beaded costume and a short dark bob. All of the other prisoners were gorgeous trained dancers who sang about how they'd committed murders, counterfeited money, robbed banks, and exacted revenge. They danced together in the jail yard, leaped over picnic tables during their recreation period, and possibly danced on cars. I knew I was mixing the film *Fame* with *Chicago*, but it was my fantasy, dammit.

I bragged about this letter to all of my friends. I carried it in my purse with me wherever I went for the next two days in a manila folder as proof of my newly found street cred. I was so tempted to write back, establish a correspondence with Catalin, bring her brownies, nail files baked in cakes, and fine lingerie sewn into stuffed animal heads. I wanted to know more.

My friend, Lucy, a dominatrix and professional Bettie Page impersonator, decided to do an Internet search on my version of Catherine Zeta-Jones. Lit cigarette dangling out of her mouth, Lucy typed Catalin's name into the Google box and hit ENTER.

Several articles came up with Catalin's name in it. I got even more excited. *Roxie Hart,* I thought, *here I come!*

"Looks like you hit the jackpot here," Lucy said, her ashes dropping onto the keyboard as we read the articles. "This is one famous bitch."

That's when things turned ugly. To my horror, we found out that Catalin, who was involved in an infamous case in the early nineties, was, in fact, a man. A forty-year-old day trader who'd lived with his mother in New York City. Apparently he'd lured a fourteen-year-old daughter of a judge to a motel, given her alcohol, had sex with her, and taped the encounter. He was the first prisoner serving a life sentence for child pornography charges. That's what happens when you target the judge's daughter (frown face).

But he never even got the sex act on tape. He only filmed for eleven minutes. The tape stopped because he forgot to rewind. This is who is sending me fan letters. An incompetent child pornographer—getting life for a sex act he didn't even get on tape. Pathetic. No wonder there were all the smiley and frown faces in the letter. He had met her on the Internet in a chat room. I wanted to throw up.

The letter took on a whole new meaning. I read it again, but instead of seeing a heavily made up moll with a dark bob and pout and beaded dress, I envisioned a sleazy, straight, middle-aged white man.

Please write back, Clarise. Eek!

Lucy thought Catalin was getting a really bad deal. She told me that fourteen was just like sixteen and that sixteen might as well be eighteen. "If you are old enough to get pregnant," she said, "you are old enough to decide whom you want to sleep with."

I reminded her that this man had lured the girl to a motel room and given her alcohol.

Lucy actually told me that he was probably good looking if he'd gotten a fourteen-year-old to come see him. He'd probably sent her a picture of himself. I wanted to smack Lucy. She then encouraged me to answer his letter to see "if there is anything there."

But then I remembered that Lucy had a high tolerance for the eccentric and insane. As a professional dom, she had clients who were kinky businessmen asking her to do things to them that most of us couldn't imagine, let alone pay for. Her primary slave at her dungeon was a Japanese businessman who would bring her four boiled eggs for each session. After giving him an enema, she'd tell him to strip naked, and then she'd shove the four eggs up his ass. Then she would call the other mistresses in and yell that he had better "lay those eggs like a good chicken!" With a very serious expression on his face, he would squawk like a chicken and lay those eggs. At the end of the hour, he'd be properly humiliated, and she'd be $300 richer and just a little more twisted.

As the years passed, I worked diligently on untwisting. And I started to notice that life was becoming less dramatic but more livable. I married a wonderful man who was stable, had a job, had never been incarcerated, and was *still* interesting. I didn't know as many people who were in life-or-death situations and didn't worry so much about myself going down the rabbit hole to uncertain depths. I didn't even associate with Lucy anymore, let alone incarcerated people I didn't know.

In the end, my lesbian love letter from prison was stripped of glamour, infused with reality, and now sits in an old filing cabinet somewhere, reminding me of where I don't want to go anymore.

Looking for My Danny Zuko

Anna David

The first boy I ever loved was named Noah. I didn't know then that Noah was also the name of the guy in the Bible story who created a brand-new world by pairing off the best of each type of animal for a boat trip followed by a civilization rebuilding. I just knew that I wanted to pair off and build a civilization with him.

Of course I didn't know what "pair off" meant, either. My understanding about sex and relationships was limited to the knowledge that, during recess, some girls guarded the Cootie Kissing Cabin while the rest of us ran off in search of boys that we could kiss and drag back there. Yet, unlike, say, a sex dungeon whose owners would confidently attach their prey to the walls and ceilings with handcuffs and stick ball gags in their mouths, we were entirely clueless about what to do with these boys once we'd caught them. So we let them go. We were not results-oriented, God bless us.

We were five.

I don't think my crush on Noah had reached full bloom until the movie *Grease* came out and by then I was eight. *Grease* was my alpha and my omega, my raison d'être before I knew people had those, even though I understood very little about what happened in it. I knew that Sandy was pretty, whether she was the innocent girl she seemed to genuinely be or had transformed into the bad "dream girl" in the skintight black pants—but I did understand that the tight black pants version of her was more exciting. In the tight black pants, she danced and smoked cigarettes and went on the Ferris wheel and was totally in with Rizzo, while when her hair was straight and she wore those long skirts, Rizzo was mean to her and Frenchie was her only friend and she coughed really hard if she tried to smoke a cigarette.

The entire subplot of the movie, where Rizzo thinks she's pregnant but then it turns out to be a false positive, was lost on me, mostly because I didn't know then that what two teenagers did in a car could result in a pregnancy; and when Kenickie called a condom his "twenty-five-cent insurance policy" and explained that he'd bought it in the seventh grade, I thought it was an actual insurance policy, and though I didn't understand why someone would need one, I figured I would by the time I got to seventh grade. (I also thought Thunder Road, where the somewhat-boring-to-me car race happens, was Dunderow.)

The character I probably related to the most was Marty, because she was a romantic (she sprayed her letters with perfume) and she knew enough to saddle up to the pseudo-famous host of the dance instead of hanging out with the high school boys. Cha-Cha, who stole Danny away at the big dance, dated the crater-faced hood whose car seemed to have flames coming out of it, terrified me. Rizzo terrified me as well. No matter how many times I saw *Grease*—and I saw *Grease* so many times that its dialogue became more familiar to me than my own thoughts—these women did not stop terrifying me.

But my focus, really, was on Sandy and Danny. The scene that is stuck in my head, probably for life, and the one I often spontaneously "perform" for people whether they like it or not, is the one when Sandy and Danny first discover that they're in the same school after the game. It goes like this (and though I cannot "do" accents to save my life, my obsession with *Grease* supersedes my inability to accent, so I can go full Australian during Sandy's dialogue in the following exchange):

Sandy: Danny?

Danny: Sandy? I thought you were going back to
Australia!

Sandy: We had a change in plans!

Danny: (*seeing the T-Birds witnessing this*): That's
cool, baby, that's cool. You know how it is.
Rockin' and rollin' and whatnot.

Sandy: (*confused*): Danny?

Danny: That's my name, baby, don't wear it out.

Sandy: What happened to the Danny Zuko I met at
the beach?

Danny: I don't know. Maybe there's two of us. Why
don't you take out a missing persons ad or
check the Yellow Pages, I don't know.

Sandy: You're a fake and a phony and I wish I'd
never laid eyes on you!

From third through sixth grade, there was a lot
of "playing *Grease*" with my friends, where I would
always make a female friend play Danny while I relished
my role of Sandy, and we would pretend the fireplace
in my house was the entrance to the fun house mirror
thing at the school fair that Sandy and Danny dance on
top of. And somehow, John Travolta and Noah meshed
in my head, though one was a Hollywood actor and
the other an innocent little boy who knew nothing of

Scientology or weird secrets—though, to be fair, they did both have excellent singing voices.

Here's the thing about my crush on Noah, or maybe this is true of all crushes at that age: we were *all* "in love with" Noah. True, there was a dearth of cute boys at my school; we were overrun with smart, nerdy kids and not future Brad Pitts. But Noah wasn't exactly in danger of one day taking Ryan Gosling's career, either. He was very sweet and had a nice smile and was smart, which I guess is to say that at the age of five, I had much better values and qualities I prioritized in romantic partners than I do today. But, anyway, we all liked him and that was totally fine because it somehow bonded us rather than making us hate each other. Because there was no end result. Much like with the Cootie Kissing Cabin, none of us would know what to do with Noah if we got him, so we could all like him together, like it was some sort of group project.

By fifth grade, things had started to get a little more complicated. Fifth grade is when I remember Cindy complimenting me on my hair color, calling it "golden" and asking if Noah liked golden hair. Her tone suggested that the competition was *on*. Fifth grade is also when I came up with the idea of calling Noah on the phone. All I remember is that I drew a picture of a phone and then wrote out what I planned to say and showed it to my mom. I don't remember if I ever went through with it but I do recall that liking Noah had started to get stressful. But the final nail in the Noah coffin happened during my birthday party that year, which took place at Great America, which was a lot like the last scene in *Grease* but it was even bigger and there were more rides and it wasn't a high school but an actual amusement park. At one point, I think during lunch and before cake, I took one of my friends aside to discuss a particular nuance of something Noah had said or done and we were deep into the analysis of What It All Meant when we realized Noah was hiding right by us and listening. Shortly afterward—perhaps minutes later—my crush on him evaporated. Somehow, like shoplifting, my love for Noah lost all its magic once it was discovered.

By seventh grade, I'd found a far safer way to protect the anonymity of a crush: by getting one on a *celebrity*. Noah still went to my school but I'd stopped even noticing, so consumed was I by my focus on an actor named C. Thomas Howell—or Tommy Howell to the readers of *Teen Beat* magazine, which you'd better believe included me. Tommy was in *The Outsiders* alongside a whole bunch of far more crush-worthy guys like Rob Lowe, Ralph Macchio, Matt Dillon, and even this dude with seriously fucked-up teeth who had the weird-sounding name of Tom Cruise. But Tom Howell was my focus, and when I say he was my focus I mean that my entire wall was covered with photos of this good- but not great-looking fellow—a bit of a Noah, really—who would go on to some degree of fame in the entirely racist movie *Soul Man* and continue working as an actor but who never found the mainstream success I always felt he deserved.

Still, my adolescent yearnings were nearly incomprehensible to me. My hormones were joining together with my innate talent not only to fantasize but also to believe those fantasies would come true so long as I strategized, controlled, and willed them to with enough fervor. They needed a place to focus and for whatever reason the home they found was Tom Howell. I didn't connect any of this to the super fun secret activity I'd discovered, which involved rubbing one of my old stuffed animals or a slipper or whatever I could find between my legs until I felt like I was being tickled to death in the most delightful way imaginable.

I also didn't know then that I was setting a pattern in place that I would end up following for the next few decades—that I was teaching myself to make up entire personalities and relationships based solely on glimmers of information combined with a whole lot of denial. In other words, what I had with Tom Howell, along with some unhealthy lessons I'd picked up along the way, gave me all the skills I needed to later get into relationships with men who were sometimes but not always terrible and then be shocked when they revealed themselves to not be the fantasy I'd created for them. Through my "relationship" with Tommy—and later, my determination to avoid reality at all costs—I somehow learned to view romance as a bright, shiny escape from reality rather than something related to mutual love and support. I can't blame Tom Howell for this, seeing as he never knew I existed, but from that situation forward, I learned to work hard in all things romance-related to maintain a fantasy persona—what my own *Teen Beat* magazine glossy might have looked like. I didn't know then that this, along with some other unhealthy lessons I'd pick up along the way, would end up temporarily eradicating nearly all of my self-esteem.

All I knew was that I was having what I perceived to be extremely emotional reactions to Tommy Howell's photos. I took my relationship with him quite seriously, penning very earnest notes (that I recently discovered) to a friend who also loved him about how another friend was only *pretending* to like him but clearly didn't have the true devotion that we did. The only wrinkle in my love for Tom Howell came when I developed feelings for another Tom: Tom Bailey, the lead singer of the Thompson Twins, who shaved his eyebrows and sang about wanting to be held now. I must have thought that since they shared a first name, this extracurricular crush sort of fit right in with my primary one. I remember crying with an emotion I thought was love at a Thompson Twins concert—kneeling, weeping, my arms reaching out through the bars of a balcony like I was grasping for God—and Stephen (who'd asked me to go steady in the fifth grade, and we had, despite my feelings for Noah, but who was now just a friend) telling me that I reminded him of a photo he'd seen of a crazed Beatles fan who he was pretty sure had been put in a mental asylum.

Years after high school, when I was in college and driving up to Tahoe, I stopped at a gas station where I ran into the boy who had started it all: Noah. He was going through what could only be described as a biblical stage then, with hair and beard and mustache so long that I wondered if he'd in fact been growing them out since I'd stopped paying attention to him in the sixth grade. The five-year-old in me was horrified by what her dream boy had turned into and was quite grateful, all those years later, that the Cootie Kissing Cabin had been a place of such nonaction. By then, I was well into my fantasy relationships with beautiful, sometimes terrible people, and wondered what I could have been thinking, at five, six, seven, eight, and nine, to have loved this earnest, strange-seeming boy so much. By then, I'd realized that it was "bad" Sandy who was on the *Grease* poster, "bad" Sandy that everyone wanted to be for Halloween. By then, in other words, becoming the fantasy held a lot more appeal than the rather creepy notion of being who I really was, especially when the only real example I had of someone being who they really were was standing in front of me holding a gas pump and looking and smelling like he hadn't showered in a while.

I was a long way, in other words, from figuring out who it was I wanted to pair off and build a civilization with, if I wanted to build a civilization with anyone at all. I'm closer to figuring all of that out today. And at least now I know that whoever he is, he's not going to need me to curl my hair and dress up in tight black pants and a leather jacket to realize he loves me.

Teenage Dream

Emma Straub

A few years ago, God gave me a birthday present. Joey McIntyre was coming to Madison, Wisconsin, four days before my twenty-seventh birthday. My boyfriend and I bought tickets the day they went on sale, and when I looked at the stubs in my hand, I saw that we had just purchased numbers one and two.

At the height of their popularity, Joey McIntyre and his bandmates from New Kids on the Block sold millions of records and played sold-out concerts around the globe, and I had the cheesy merchandise to show for it. I had NKOTB bedsheets, two sets of dolls (one each in concert outfits and street wear), life-sized cardboard cutouts, posters, trading cards, earrings, buttons, novelizations, comic books, a coffee-table-sized collection of photographs, and a fanny pack. I was a Blockhead. It wasn't that I thought they'd made perfect music—some of the Kids had better voices than others, let's be honest. But my Joey—he was good. During the band's golden years, Joey hadn't yet gone through puberty, and the high, clear tone of his voice was as beautiful as a choir of angels, if the angels happened to be from the Boston suburbs.

I had seen Joey in person twice before. When I was eight years old and at the height of my devotion, the band appeared in the Macy's Thanksgiving Day Parade, riding down the street on a float shaped like a Red Delicious apple. There are two photographs taken of me that day: the first is a blurry shot of the side of my face, my mouth hanging open in disbelief as I see Joey for the first time. I am unaware of the photographer (my mother, no doubt), or of anyone else near me (which must have included everyone in New York City). Seeing Joey live, in tender, human flesh, completely took my breath away, and I look like Saint Theresa, pierced by Joey's falsetto. The next photograph in the series shows me scowling directly into the lens, after Joey has moved on with his float, as if in doing so he has broken up with me. The fact that he was gone, and I knew he wasn't coming back, ruined my mood for the rest of the day, if not the rest of the month.

The second time I saw him was more than ten years later, when I was home from college. Joey was on tour supporting his first solo record, and I went to the concert alone, after friends told me that, if I wanted them to come, I would have to pay for their tickets and an additional sum in order to make it worth their while. I was surrounded by women my own age, all of us more or less adults, all of us more or less pretending we were there out of some nostalgic curiosity. When the lights went out to signal that Joey was about to come on stage, I screamed, losing my voice in the chorus of screams around me. The sound was completely involuntary and came from a part of my psyche so deep that I had genuinely forgotten that it was there.

Before the show in Madison, I was consumed with anxiety. My best friend sent me heart-shaped NKOTB earrings for my birthday, and I was wearing them, which made me feel both loyal and a little bit guilty. I didn't want Joey to think I was one of those girls who only loved him for his past—I was there for contemporary Joey, Joey 2007, whose tour blog declared that his (self-released) record was made up of jazz standards.

There was a line outside the Orpheum when my boyfriend Mike and I arrived. I'm not used to being the thinnest person in any group, so I was surprised to see that Joey's fans seemed to have increased in body size, if not number. Mike gave nods to the few other gentlemen who had escorted their ladies and then tried his best to blend into the side of the building.

My fellow fans were, on the whole, female, white, and hovering somewhere in their thirties. Each one had a camera in her lap and drummed her fingers nervously. I snagged two seats in the front row while Mike went to the bathroom. My rough head count clocked eighty people; the room fit three hundred. When I was in elementary school, at the apex of my devotion, I was one of only a small handful of devotees among my classmates. It was neither cool nor uncool to love the New Kids; it was just My Thing. Now I found myself in a room packed with heavy, suburban-looking women, wearing flowery tunic tops and too much hairspray, women I would normally think that I had nothing in common with. We shared something so deep and profound that I wanted to throw my arms around each of them, which, after all, wouldn't have taken more than about fifteen minutes. I struck up conversations with everyone I made eye contact with, and we were all buzzing with excitement. Finally: a sisterhood.

Mike came back looking stricken.

"What happened?" I asked him.

"There were two girls in the bathroom," he said, "and one of them said, 'I don't care if we have to double-team him, I'm not leaving here without getting some.'" I bought him a drink.

The house band—keyboards, drums, guitar, and upright bass—came on stage first. Joey trotted out with a smile, treating the stage as though it were larger than ten feet by six feet. He was dressed in a narrow black suit, complete with vest, and a matching fedora, stylishly askew. We swooned.

Joey started the show with a Nat King Cole song. He danced around the stage, snapping his fingers and using the mic stand as a dance partner. The applause, much to my surprise, was tepid. This did not escape Joey's attention.

"Google Nat King Cole," he told us. "It's good music for necking." Then he repeated the word "necking" a few times, realizing that it sounded odd. I laughed. Joey was funny. This was something I hadn't seen before; in all the gloss and costumes, even the clasped, outstretched hands, there had been precious little human interaction. This Joey in front of me was more interesting. He had a gigantic, pulsing, throbbing chip on his shoulder.

His stage banter got weirder as the concert progressed. Despite the aforementioned heft of the audience members, Joey seemed taken by our attractiveness. "Where were you back then?" he asked, referring to the group's heyday. "You were babies. Babies! With enormous buttons." Joey did an impression of a baby with a Flavor Flav–sized button around

202 True Tales of Lust & Love

its neck, weighing it down, complete with "goo goo ga ga" noises. The crowd laughed. We knew how big the buttons were; we'd all had them. "Why couldn't you switch places? Back then, you were babies, I couldn't do anything about it, and now I'm married." Marriage seemed to be a touchy issue for Joey. Before playing "My Funny Valentine," he launched into the murky waters of extramarital temptations. "It's okay to look," he said. "You can get right up to the point, right up to the point"—here he used his hands to show us his two palms nearly touching—"as long as nothing happens, it's not a sin." We all knew Joey was raised Catholic, the youngest of nine children. We all understood where he was coming from. According to Wikipedia, Joey was the first person on MTV's show *Cribs* to enter his bedroom and say, "This is where the magic happens."

During the ballads, women would shyly get up from their seats and walk in pairs down the aisles in order to get a better picture. While most of the women were in dressy tops and jeans, one woman wore a 1940s-style dress and danced in the aisle. Joey clearly liked her best. Every time someone took a picture, Joey would turn his face toward the camera without actually acknowledging the photo being taken. This seemed all well and good until Joey did the inevitable and sang "Please Don't Go Girl," the song that launched a million first crushes, not to mention the song that I lip-synched at my tenth birthday party. Women gasped, then shrieked, then tried not to sing along at full volume. I took a thirty-second video with my camera, swaying in time with the music. The high notes weren't as high, but the song seemed more plausible now, more authentic. Joey could have been singing to an actual person. He could have written the song himself. It's unusual for me, as an adult who has zero interest in professional sports, to be in a room surrounded by people who are deeply moved simultaneously, and I felt woozy with connection.

Even after the New Kids on the Block song, our dearest and dirtiest wish come true, some of my fellow Blockheads were still not sated. Two women sitting at a table near the stage called out requests for more New Kids songs. Joey demurred, first politely, and then with more force. "What do you want me to sing, fucking 'Popsicle'? Fuck you!" This was when Joey started to swear at the audience.

"Popsicle" is a song on the very first New Kids record, released in 1986, when Joey was fourteen years old. "Fuck you!" Joey had seen his window of opportunity open and close. The crowd had turned. My boyfriend began to laugh, delighted that he was finally getting a show. I covered my mouth with my hands. Who were these girls, who would taunt our Joey so? I would have politely clapped through Irish step dancing, through magic tricks, through Tuvan throat singing. I wanted to muzzle the noisiest girls, to shut their mouths so that Joey would never know he hadn't been a smash hit. "How many of you think I'm crazy?" Joey asked. Several people in the audience raised their hands.

The girls in the bathroom were right; sexual encounters were there to be had, if one understood the rules about temptation and intercourse. Joey was teetering on the edge, a place he'd likely been for years, since his first solo record. He wanted us to love him; no, he needed us to love him, enough to put up with our middling applause for the songs he wanted to sing. That was when I realized that what I felt for Joey was empathy. I'd known him so long, more than half my life. It was my dolls and buttons—my voice screaming at the Macy's Thanksgiving Day Parade—that made it impossible for him to find any other career path satisfying. On stage, Joey tried to block us out and nodded his head as the other musicians soloed, snapping his fingers in time with the music. He was done with us.

I own a well-worn VHS copy of "Hangin' Tough Live," a concert video shot when Joey was a prepubescent teenager. In it, he skates along the surface of interaction with his fans, smiling up toward the lights. He keeps his distance from the screaming crowd, even while performing his pelvic thrusts, leaving it to Donnie Wahlberg to really wink at the fans, to smile, to suggest he might like to take the prettiest girl backstage and have his way with her. Joey, on the other hand, looks like an angelic child, his voice high and sweet, his movements gangly and boyish. At the time, Joey seemed to me to be a man, but he wasn't. I'd had no idea.

Despite all of this, there was no way I was going to miss the meet and greet. The curtain had been pulled back, and we had all seen the wizard. No one was going to leave now. How many opportunities would I have to see Joey so close up? Surely he would recover. And true enough, ten minutes after the show was over, Joey wound his way through the mostly empty theater and took his spot in the lobby. Every woman still there got in line, and, one by one, we got our pictures taken and our CDs signed. While we waited, I agonized over what to say once he was standing in front of me. I thought about telling Joey that his birthday remains my ATM pin number, but decided that was too creepy.

By the time Mike and I reached the table, my entire body was vibrating. I know I hugged him, and I remember the satin back of his vest, and how blue his eyes were, but little else comes back to me. Even though I was aware that my reaction—compassion, affection, horror, pity—was complicated, the fact of Joey's physical body in my arms made me quiver with excitement. Still scrambling for something to say, I offered the cringe-worthy "I even brought my boyfriend!" Joey, generous in the moment, looked toward Mike and then back at me, already resigned to hearing such sentences for the rest of his life. "You really owe him," Joey said. I felt terrible. And yet, I had touched Joey. Joey had touched me. There was photographic proof. There was something about the longevity of my love for Joey that made it legitimate. Joey might be crazy, but I was, too. My heartbeat didn't return to normal for several hours, maybe even a full day.

Almost exactly a year after the concert in Madison, Joey and the rest of the New Kids appeared on the *Today* show, officially announcing their reunion. The segment begins with Meredith Vieira and Natalie Morales standing outside the studio in the dripping rain. Thousands of fans line the metal barricades, many of them wearing New Kids T-shirts, hats, and the aforementioned dinner-plate-sized buttons. A giant red curtain falls, and there are the New Kids, all five of them, just standing there, like animals in a zoo.

"And what can we expect from the New Kids this time around?" Meredith asks.

"Three things," Joey says. "The economy, health care, and job security." He shakes his head, still unable to believe that he has committed himself to live this life all over again. "Long live the Block." The hosts laugh politely and throw it back to Al Roker, on location outside a motel in Memphis, Tennessee. It is also the

fortieth anniversary of Martin Luther King Jr.'s assas-
sination. Roker has a brief, solemn exchange with Al
Sharpton before going back to Vieira and Joey and the
New Kids, still mugging for the crowd and each other.
Joey's mouth is already open in the same practiced smile
I'd seen him make over and over again. Danny's face
has mysterious lines. Donnie's hairline is a memory.
Jordan smiles dumbly and wanders slightly out of the
frame. Did Joey really have to share a dressing room
with Jordan Knight again? Some fates did seem more
cruel than obscurity. The crowd, as zealous as ever,
doesn't flinch.

It can't be a coincidence that the reunion came soon
after the concert I saw. In my imagination, it was that
one night that broke the camel's back. Joey had seen
the alternative route, the small crowds and tepid cheers,
and he had made a choice. His was not going to be the
life of an artist, with room for growth and change over
time. Joey's life was going to be static, frozen in place.
The money would be better, but I'm sure that wasn't
the issue. The decision that Joey had made was simple:
it was better to be adored, no matter the cost.

Dr. Carlisle

Fielding Edlow

*T*his is a love story about my OB/GYN, who looks like a prettier, less drunk version of Belinda Carlisle at the height of the Go-Go's. I will refer to her as Dr. Carlisle.

My first shrink really liked the idea of a "pretty doctor." When my acting career was relegated to angry feminist community theater, like playing the well-meaning but conflicted Belle in *Vulvalution: Her Lips Speak*, my shrink and I had a serious talk. One day she lit up like a Jungian Lite-Brite. "Acting really doesn't seem to be working out for you. What about med school? You could be a pretty doctor!" I remember thinking, *That's kind of sexist*, but then I got excited because my next thought was, *Oh my God, she thinks I'm pretty!* Dr. Metzger was a fairly good shrink. She got me off coke, Prozac, Nutter Butters, and blowing losers in the bathroom of Dorrian's, an Upper East Side bar made famous for having been the place where the Preppy Murderer and his victim were before they went to Central Park. But years later, I really just remember three things she said: Don't do caffeine after 2:00 PM; "No" is a complete sentence; and Openly eating cake batter while walking down the street does not constitute a meal.

My OB/GYN is so pretty that when I stand next to her, I feel like a small, hairy, Jewish Minotaur. She's so pretty that my brother—who's a neurologist at Harvard—got furious when I showed him her picture. "Are you fucking kidding me? Is she even board certified? What's wrong with you and why does it look like there's a wind machine on her hair?" She does have this glossy, Pre-Raphaelite chestnut brown hair that flips up insouciantly at the ends and always seems to say, "I'm perfect. Go fuck yourself." I didn't understand how my brother didn't want to fuck her, too—although his anger seemed to suggest that maybe he secretly did. Her face is like a silky banyan tree or a Greek sunset or a tiramisu that makes you skinny.

I was nervous before meeting Dr. Carlisle because my friends had told me how pretty she was. But they also were very clear with me. "Don't get sucked in because she's *not* perfect. She wasn't in the cool group in high school, and she's not funny." I remember sitting in her turquoise blue waiting room, which felt like a fairy's aquarium, and sniffing her fig hand soap on my fingers. I remember discovering her middle name on one of the degrees on her wall and feeling like we belonged together. I was very intrigued by this Beverly Hills doctor who didn't take insurance and who *chose* to bury her face in pussy all day. I was a dyke for a month and I didn't do it. Most girls, when they decide to have a gay phase, have just gotten totally fucked over by some horrible guy, had a keg of Jägermeister, and said, "Fuck it! Let's go munch a million boxes at Meow Mix!" I was three days sober and thought, *Wait a second, do I want backstage passes to Lilith Fair?* But let me tell you a little something: no amount of San Pellegrino is going to make me wanna munch box.

When Dr. Carlisle walked in, I jumped like a horny J-date. I felt immediate shame in front of her. I was sure Dr. Carlisle never felt shame—never publicly binged on Duncan Hines yellow cake mix and had probably never gotten fingered in Row P during an INXS concert. During the appointment, she asked me if I was interested in getting pregnant. I examined her to see if she wanted me to or not.

"Well, I'm not really ready yet," I said. "I kinda wanna be more established in my career. I know I'm in my middle-late thirties but—"

She cut me off. "You seem very wise and I'm sure when you try, you'll have no problem since you have a great attitude about it."

I wanted it to start drizzling and for her two dumber-than-fuck assistants to shut down the office so we could curl up together and read *Island of the Blue Dolphins*.

When I got home that night, I told my husband, Larry, that we should wait to get pregnant. My emotionally unstable actor husband, who's an exact cross between an Irish splinter group and a whispery ballerina, had a hissy fit. "What the fuck?! I'm *old*. I knew you didn't want to have kids. Fuck you, Fielding! Family is the *most important* thing. Your eggs are probably toxic and dead anyway!" Then, a second later, "Will you come to Yogurtland with me?"

I got pregnant two months later, thanks to the iPhone app FemCal Lite and my B+ in Biology of Women at U Penn. FemCal Lite told me the exact day when Larry should jizz inside me. It was a bright morning in June and Larry was putting on his man sandals and stapling his pic and résumés together in the most annoying way when I stopped him. "I need you to come home later—and can you try to not jerk off today? Or at least not *again*?"

"What? I don't know if I can, I have a call back for *Suburgatory*."

"I need you to come home after the stupid audition and dump a load in me."

"I'll dump a load in you."

"Great, and can you also pick up two bags of kitty litter on your way back?"

When I got the official "You're pregnant" three-minute voice mail message from Dr. Carlisle, I immediately treated six people to lattes in Starbucks. And so our dating began, with my eye always on our looming hospital consummation. But Larry was onto me, especially since he was discovering mounds of cut pubic hair all over the bathroom sink (it's rude not to trim before visits). He even insisted on coming with me to my five-month checkup.

As we sat in her office, I watched Larry get completely sucked in by her sea green Manolos, silk miniskirt, and seductive fig waft. It was during that visit that Dr. Carlisle attempted a joke. "So I'd start having sex now 'cause it's going to be a bit challenging later on," she said with a smile. I guess it wasn't really a joke. But, desperate for more intimacy snippets from her, I said, "Yeah, Larry's not that interested—he thinks he's gonna dent the baby's head with his cock." Awkward silence.

I wanted to tell her that the one time we fucked, it took forty-five minutes for me to climb on top and when I did, Larry told me I was breathing like John Goodman. I wanted her to know that I couldn't do any of the tricks I could when I was fifty pounds lighter: I couldn't bend down and be like, "Do you like it?" or inquire, "How wet is my pussy?" Because that's rhetorical anyway: your pussy is always wet when you're pregnant. I wanted to be able to tell her that my poor little portal was trapped beneath my big fat fucking pregnancy gut, like James Franco's arm in *127 Hours*, and that my daughter was going to enter a world with a lot of closed doors, sticky iPads, and secrets.

After another of my appointments, Larry spotted my sparkly Louboutins under the couch and said, "Tell me you didn't wear your wedding shoes to the checkup." Silence. "You do know that when you give birth, you're probably gonna take a big shit in front of her face."

He was right: I did poop a couple of times during the birth. I sort of knew it but each time I just kind of pretended I was in a blackout. Aside from that, I had a gorgeous shiny-haired nymph's hands in me—massaging, cajoling my stubborn daughter out with her goddessy mineral oil, form-fitting scrubs, and festive Nikes.

It was the first time I heard her say my name. I couldn't have cared less about my daughter coming out. I just wanted to hear, "*Yes,* Fielding, beautiful Fielding, that's it, Fielding!" But I only got that when I had a good push and my husband was very clear with me that, during the first hour, my pushes were very general and *not* good. So I ended up pushing for four hours—not to try to avoid a cesarean or to have some transcendent, spiritual experience with my daughter. No. I just wanted Dr. Carlisle's hands in me—sweet-talking my lazy daughter, who had obviously set up some sort of cozy night lounge in my uterus.

The evening before I delivered, Dr. Carlisle broke my water wearing a fur vest and UGGs after having just finished up a steak dinner at Mastro's with her Persian husband. I still remember exactly how it felt when she stuck her manicured hand up inside me and, with the flick of a finger, broke my water. My cervix was stubborn. But my small warm river gushed over her Seven jeans and it was foreplay at its best. Yes, she doesn't take insurance, and it's true that she's not very theatrical and was borderline anticlimactic when she announced, "It's a girl." And yeah, she's not that funny. But she cried a little when my daughter was born. And the next day, when the roads around Cedars were blocked off because of the L.A. marathon, *she ran with the marathoners* in order to make my follow-up visit and arrived in a sporty tracksuit. But the most meaningful moment in our entire relationship occurred the night before I gave birth, when she was examining me and my daughter reached out and grabbed her hand like she was shaking it. Because that's when I learned that my daughter, Ellis, at 0, had more poise, boundaries, and professionalism than I did at thirty-seven.

Phatso

Iris Smyles

To think that I've wasted years of my life, that I've longed to die, that I've experienced my greatest love, for a woman who didn't even appeal to me, who wasn't even my type.

—Marcel Proust, *Swann's Way*

The ace of spades shows a naked woman reclining on a desk with her legs opening upward as if to embrace the sky. In her right hand she holds a book—*The Collected Poems of Mallarmé*, I imagine, though the title is out of focus. With her left, she adjusts her reading glasses. In other words, she's "bookish."

Years ago, growing bored of bottle caps and pencil erasers, I started collecting pornography. My collection features a book of 3-D nudes, the Tijuana bibles, a few instruction manuals with illustrations—*Total Sexual Fitness for Women* offers exercises I can practice by myself—two fetish DVDs with lots of spanking but no sex at all, and five sets of dirty playing cards ranging in theme from Ancient Greek Lovers to the more contemporary Poke-her, from which I've pulled the ace.

It's natural to identify with the characters in novels and movies, and so I identify with the figures in porn. Because I'm not sure what "type" of woman I am, however, I generally end up trying to squeeze into the closest fit. As a child I related to Cinderella, for example, though clearly she and I had nothing in common. She was an underprivileged blonde left always to tend the hearth; I was a gawky brunette enrolled in ballet school and accustomed to central heating. Still, despite my knowing I wasn't right for the part, I cast myself in the role anyway.

My new boyfriend Glen says he's into bookish women, but I think he just likes librarian-themed pornography. "You're exactly my type," he told me on our first date. Since we met in a bookstore, I'd assumed he was bookish too, and was excited to play up that aspect of my character. I'd imagined a brilliant first date conversation in which we'd debate the finer points of Henry James's later work and had even prepared an inappropriate joke about James's testicular injuries, which I planned to trot out over dessert to show my lighter side.

As it turned out, my prepping was in vain. Glen had wandered into the bookstore only to buy coffee and had little or no appetite for the books themselves, he confessed. This was a disappointment, though it did little to lessen my attraction to him ultimately, as I noticed he had a remarkably hairy chest. A veritable beast, he was, judging from the wild tangle springing ferociously from the top of his V-neck. It thrilled me to imagine myself Boof to his Teen Wolf, while he busily imagined himself student to my teacher. "I love your sweater vest," he said over dessert. And then, just a few dates later, we adopted two new roles: a young man and a young woman at the start of a great romance.

I didn't mind being reduced to a type. That he managed to flatten my whole personality in order to meet the demands of his fetish was exciting. I belonged to a category and also to him. I've always enjoyed being objectified, specifically being called by pet diminutives like "baby" or "doll." It's not so uncommon, this desire to become small, to be furnished with sensible handles by which one might more easily be held.

Eager to reciprocate, I told Glen he was my type, too. Bringing the back of one of his furry hands to my face, I told him that I loved his flaxen knuckle curls and began waxing romantic about his type's recurrence in the novels of H.G. Wells. I described how I imagined him long before we met, naked, running through the forest shrouded in dense fog, pursued by trappers, nearly escaping. And then, a tangle of nets, and another, now a cage, inside of which he is delivered to civilization, to a secret lab just outside of London, where an evil genius performs ungodly experiments on him, injecting him daily with a mysterious serum that bestows humanoid characteristics upon him and gives him some, but not all, of man's higher brain functions. "And with the injection of this daily serum," I told him excitedly, "your body has miraculously transformed into the human shape that now sits before me. Glen!" I cried. "Your hands are a vestige of the savage beast within you, the beast which I adore!"

Glen asked me what "serum" meant and, pulling his hand away, asked me to stop making fun of him. Reluctantly I released his paw and took out my stop-watch to time his beard growth while we waited for appetizers.

I don't really have a "type" myself, but have over the years cast a variety of men in the role of prince. To me, this is proof of my being open-minded; to my friends, it's just evidence of my fetishism. My dating a man of forty-two when I was eighteen indicated, they asserted, an "avuncular fetish." And my dating a carnie one summer out on Coney Island made apparent, they said, my "toothless fetish." And then, when in college I happened to date a few fat guys, they dubbed me "chubby-chaser."

This one ex-boyfriend was so fat that when he lay on top of me I feared being crushed, snapped in two, like a twig on the forest floor in James Fenimore Cooper's *Leatherstocking Tales*. After our first night together, he pulled me in close. "See how I mold perfectly to your body? If I were thin, there would be all this space between us. I don't want there to be any space between us," he whispered. I was touched by his argument's persuasiveness and could genuinely appreciate his flab curving into the small of my back when we spooned. It was like being encased in bubble wrap. I felt very secure. Like a very delicate plate being transported overseas via superior postage.

I very quickly came to enjoy the look of him too. How he was planet-like, I'd think, as he exhaled rings of marijuana smoke, which wreathed him like Saturn. And there I was next to him in the kitchen, barefoot and so tiny by comparison, his little moon. I began to think of physical attraction in a whole new way. He was a large physical mass with its own powerful gravitational pull—making it quite natural, quite inevitable, really, that I should fall for or into him.

Phatso and I had fun all the time. No one ever made me laugh the way that he did, and his were the most skillful penis puppet shows I've seen. And I've seen a lot. I don't know if this is something most couples share, or if there is something unique to my "type" that inspires men to invest their penises with stage names and perform, but for me it happens regularly. Nearly all of my serious boyfriends have at one point or another erected such presentations. It would never do to ask if this was their first time, or if there were girlfriends before me with whom they had rehearsed. "But that," as Rudyard Kipling would say, "is another story."

Phatso had been a moderately successful comedian before he decided one winter—the one of our discontent—that he wanted to act. Returning from his agent's office on a gray afternoon, he told me what his agent had just told him: as he looked at the time, he'd be too difficult to cast. He'd need to either gain or lose weight to fit a "type." Did he want to be a character actor, or compete for leading man roles?

Fatter sounded good to me and I told him. "Roles are rolls," I said, my hand drifting unconsciously toward his gut, where it stuck against his shirt like an ecstatic ten-year-old pasted to the wall of a Gravitron ride. I gave him a squeeze, raised an eyebrow, and nodded toward the bedroom.

He didn't see himself that way, he answered. He wanted to be a leading man, and took off for the kitchen to continue the conversation over soda and Hot Pockets. He took off—and without noticing, released my hand back into space like a bottle of Coca-Cola Classic in that commercial from 1985. I caught up to him by the microwave where he was already punching in numbers. After a moment he turned around and looked at me with tears in his eyes. The timer beeped, like "Taps."

Later that afternoon we rented *Fatso* with Dom

DeLuise. We sat on the couch, and I stroked his hair and fed him Devil Dogs while he cried. He began his diet and exercise regimen the next day, and a month later he was muscular and thin. He took to eating soy, got his hair spiked at a salon and, I don't know, it was as if his whole personality had disappeared with his chins. Suddenly he wasn't fat and stupid, which had been a disarmingly sexy combination, but just average-looking and stupid, which was not sexy at all. The man I loved, it seemed, had been pissed away in water weight.

After that I found someone fatter. Really fat. His body was a true extravagance. Breaking up is always hard. But perhaps he, with all his padding, might make for a softer rebound. My friends nicknamed Phatso's sequel "Type 2," short for "Type 2 Diabetes." More romantically, I nicknamed him "The Love Barge." And whether by his side or taken up into the berth of his great arms, like a dinghy attached to a monstrous ocean vessel, when I was with him I felt so marvelously small.

It was at a bar where all my friends drank regularly that he kissed me for the first time. We'd been flirting all night when, instead of flashing a bewitching smile like I'd meant to, I accidentally threw up a shot of Jägermeister. (Later, I found out he had a fetish for young alcoholics.) Quickly, I covered my mouth. I was so embarrassed.

And so I ran, like Cinderella at midnight, while he, obese prince, panted after me down the steps and into the men's urinal where, letting my upchuck burst into full flower, I had just enough time to rinse my mouth out in the sink. A moment later Type 2 caught up to me. Wheezing at my back, he spun me around and took me in his arms, and giving me a look like the Jack of hearts, he kissed me.

My Very Own Stripper

Laura House

*I*n 2006, I got the most exciting awesome job a writer could have: a staff position on a real, live network sitcom. It was really different from the job I had just before that—working at a private Orthodox yeshiva.

This job had incredible perks, like craft service, an amazing paycheck, and, my second week there, a trip to Vegas. Why? Just for fun. Because that's what rich people do. It's also what people who like strippers do. And my boss happened to be both.

This almost never happened at the yeshiva.

I had very little experience with strippers. As a comic in Austin, I'd seen guys date them. And there always seemed to be one hanging around the comedy club because she thought she was funny. I'd been to Sugar's in Austin. It was a midlevel strip club. Girls danced while guys ate. It just seemed like a weird McDonald's—like, usually there's a playground with a fun slide but at this one there were seminaked ladies dancing on a pole. Whatever. Either way, enjoy the fries.

In Vegas we stayed at the Venetian and I roomed with the only other female writer, Martha. We worked for about an hour in the head writer's room so we could officially call it a work trip, then we were off. We hit the pool, did some gambling, ate at Tao. This was so much better than working at the yeshiva. Although, to be fair, Purim carnival is a hoot.

At dinner, our boss introduced us to a friend of his. I'll call her Renee, since I don't remember her name. She's his friend, who's not his wife, who lives in Vegas, and she was going to join us. "Okay, hi," we all said awkwardly. She was cute, had harsh cut bangs like his wife, sweet with really high energy. I don't want to be an armchair doctor but I'd say she was tweaking on coke. But what do I know? It could have been meth.

We met up at 10:00 PM to get in limos, with Renee leading the way. The first club was lame so we left and went to the Spearmint Rhino.

This is where my life changed and I learned things about myself that never would have come up in therapy and still don't.

We walked in to a warm welcome. My boss was

called by name and each of us was met by our very
own stripper. A very pretty woman approached me
with excitement, warmth, and sincerity. "Hi, welcome,
how are you?" she asked, looking genuinely happy
to see me. Not like a skeezy stripper but like an old
friend. As if she'd been waiting for me to show up.
She wrapped her arm in mine and led me through the
club. And, I swear, I've never had this feeling before
or since but I just wanted to hand her cash. I felt wel-
comed by this woman. I felt attractive. I felt *wanted*.
My heart opened up. I felt compassion and forgiveness
for all the guys that I'd known through the years who
had loved to go to strip bars and I'd always thought of
as losers. What I once thought of only as disgusting,
I now saw as incredibly fucking pleasant. God bless
strippers.

We were led to a really dark, semiprivate room.
Martha explained to me that she didn't want to stay
in this room because all our coworkers were about to
get private lap dances. And watching your coworkers
dry-hump strangers and come in their pants is just not
conducive to a healthy work environment.

Agreed.

And I didn't want to stay there because I couldn't see
the pole dancers.

I didn't know this was a desire I had but when we'd
first walked through the main floor, there they were

on stage, and I was fascinated. I wanted to watch the show, not get lap dances.

That's when Renee stepped in and saved the day. "You don't have to get a lap dance," she said. "Just tell the girls you want a massage. They can't legally call it that because they're not licensed but they can rub your shoulders and stuff. Just say you want a back rub."

Seriously? I loved massages! This was perfect. Move over Disneyland—the Spearmint Rhino was now the happiest place on earth.

Then my boss pulled me aside and said, "You know how this works, right? I pay for everything. Do not spend a penny. All the girls or dances, food, champagne, strawberries, whatever you want. I pay for it. Okay?" Okay. It just got more perfect.

Renee somehow knew all the ins and outs of this place. She even seemed to know some of the dancers. I can't prove it but I think she used to work there. I also think she might currently work there.

Regardless, I was glad to be friends with someone on the inside now that I was here. I really just wanted to go the main room and watch the ladies dance and get a massage and eat some strawberries. Is that weird? Of course it is.

But it was free. And it was a Thursday night and a lot better than sitting home watching *ER*.

Renee led us out into the crowded main room. The

writer guys stayed in the dark room. And our boss was taken upstairs to some especially special room that I don't like to think about.

She got us to a private booth in the back with a Ving Rhames–looking guy standing watch. She gave some kind of nod in secret stripper speak and he opened the curtain for us.

Safe! We stepped inside the booth, our own little oasis. Renee said, "Pick a girl."

I was asked to look at this sea of women and simply pick. But I couldn't. What do you mean, pick a girl? No. These are people. You can't just choose one. I'm not some kind of . . . I just wouldn't know how.

"Okay, no problem." Renee had a swig of champagne, sniffed, and said, "Don't tell your boss I'm drinking. He paid for my rehab."

Mum's the word.

She sniffed, downed some more champagne, rubbed her nose, and said, "I'll be right back."

About a nanosecond later, a stripper ran inside. Like a bug. She just scampered into our booth. She sat down and talked to us like she knew us, so for a minute I assumed she did.

She started rubbing Martha's hand and telling her about her life. And that's how Martha found her stripper.

A few minutes later, Renee showed up with five girls. For lack of a better description, one of each: there was tall/skinny/black; harsh bangs/side ponytails/ Catholic schoolgirl; short/curvy/Jessica Alba lips; big-boob blonde; and Asian.

Renee repeated the directive: pick one.

In that moment, I looked at her and these girls standing there, looking at me, each wanting to be picked. And I thought, *This is disgusting. These are women, to be respected. They aren't pieces of meat to be picked over. They aren't something I'm to choose or not choose to my whim. They are people. Humans with feelings. You don't just choose.*

In that same moment I realized, without question, which I wanted. And I pointed: HER. Right in the middle. The cute curvy one with full, pouty Jessica Alba lips.

Turns out, I have a type.

She smiled and came in, so happy to be there. Renee and the rejects scattered. I told her I'd like a back rub. She put my legs up on the seat, moved me sideways, got behind me, and dug her fingers into my tense shoulders (I had been a writer for a full week and a half!). Heaven.

I leaned back, listened to the music, watched the dancers, drank my Diet Coke, and had this hot Albanian chick, fake-named Cinnamon, rub my shoulders. My lesbo fantasy was coming true and I didn't even know I had one.

I indulged for about ten minutes before I looked over at Martha, miserable, having her hand rubbed by her chatty-ass stripper. She was barely rubbing, just going through the motions while going on and on about her boyfriend and his new truck.

Martha looked over at me, my muscles relaxing in the capable hands of my hot stripper, who spoke only rarely, to inform me that she was studying massage therapy or to ask if I wanted another sip of my drink or a strawberry.

Martha made the hopeful face with her eyebrows and switch sign with her hands. "Can we? You know? Can I have your stripper for a while?"

I didn't want to lend my stripper out to anyone—she was mine after all—but I felt bad.

So we switched.

Her bony stripper lanked over to me, and my beautiful, fit, curvy Alba-type headed over to Martha. I missed her already.

Martha's stripper talked. And talked and talked. On and on about her dumb boyfriend and his truck, all while giving me a rubdown with all the oomph of a wet noodle. And I had a thought I'd never had before. I wanted to stand and shout, "Zip it! I'm not paying you to run your trap!" I was suddenly James Caan about to backhand a working girl. I didn't, of course. But I felt the impulse and it was a first. And kind of scary. But also kind of hot! Is there no end to what I will learn about myself, Rhino?

I looked over at Martha melting under the firm grip of my sweet stripper. Now I had sad face and switched hands.

After a couple of hours, Renee came over and rounded us up—sniffing, rubbing her nose on her sleeve, and politely finishing up any of our undrunk champagne. "You guys ready to go? I think we're clearing out."

I'd done it. I'd lasted as long as the guys in the strip club.

I had actually gotten used to it. I was going to miss our private little red-curtained booth and my pretty little Alba-esque dancer. We left the comfort of the booth and were back out in the melee. It was crowded and loud. I was instantly annoyed by all the riffraff. Ugh. They weren't like us; they weren't here ironically. They were losers. We were important people, in from out of town. We had had a private booth.

Then Renee explained that the private booth cost $300 an hour. I had assumed when my boss said, "I pay for everything," that it would be like when you gave kids a roll of quarters for the arcade. But my boss calmly came over to settle up the tab, paying them a grand and tipping them an additional grand. Then he paid for everyone else. I'd never seen anything like it. Certainly not at the yeshiva. We were lucky if we found stale rugelach in the teacher's lounge. My boss spent about $20,000 that night. About what I'd made the year before.

I learned a lot that night. That I had an awesome job. That money does buy some degree of happiness. And that I'm just gay enough to thoroughly enjoy strippers.

About Our Contributors

ALISON AGOSTI has written for Rob Dyrdek's *Ridiculousness* on MTV and is a writer for the sketch team New Money, which performs a monthly show at the Upright Citizens Brigade Theatre in L.A. She is also a sketch writer for John Moe's popular radio show *Wits*, syndicated on American Public Media. Through *Wits* she has been lucky enough to write for Maria Bamford, Kristen Schaal, Dave Foley, Julia Sweeney, and John Hodgman. Alison also contributes regularly to *The Atlantic*.

SARA BARRON is the author of two essay collections, *People Are Unappealing: Even Me* (Random House, 2009) and *The Harm in Asking*, which is due out March 2014. Her work has appeared on NPR, *This*

American Life, and VanityFair.com. She's a host of the Moth StorySLAMS in New York, and she teaches humor writing at Gotham Writers' Workshop.

SARA BENINCASA is a comedian and author who has appeared on MTV, VH1, CNN, Fuse, History Channel, FX, NBC's *Today* show, CBS, Japan's TV Asahi, Russia Today TV, and Norwegian national television. Her memoir, *Agorafabulous! Dispatches from My Bedroom*, was released by William Morrow/HarperCollins in 2012. Her most recent TV credits include FX's *Totally Biased with W. Kamau Bell* and History Channel's *I Love the 1880s*. She hosts the storytelling show Family Hour with Auntie Sara at the Nerdist Showroom at Meltdown Comics in Los Angeles.

CHLOE CALDWELL is the author of the essay collection *Legs Get Led Stray*. Her nonfiction has appeared in *Salon*, *The Rumpus*, *Nylon*, *Men's Health*, and *The Sun*. She lives in Portland, Oregon.

CINDY CHUPACK is an author, storyteller, relationship columnist, and Emmy-winning comedy writer whose credits include *Modern Family, Sex and the City*, and *Everybody Loves Raymond*. Her first book, *The Between Boyfriends Book: A Collection of Cautiously Hopeful Essays*, was a *New York Times* bestseller that was translated into nine languages. She's writing and producing a pilot for Fox based on her comedic marriage memoir, *The Longest Date: Life as a Wife*, which will be released in January 2014 by Viking Press.

MEGHAN DAUM has been an opinion columnist at *Los Angeles Times* since 2005. She is the author of the essay collection *My Misspent Youth*, the novel *The Quality of Life Report*, and the memoir *Life Would Be Perfect if I Lived in That House*. She has written for numerous publications, including *The New Yorker*, *Harper's*, *The New York Times Magazine*, and *Vogue*. Learn more about her at www.meghandaum.com.

ANNA DAVIES has written about her love life for *The New York Times, Elle, Glamour, Salon*, and others, which is why she never reveals her full name until date number three with a guy. In addition to occasional oversharing, Anna has written three YA novels— *Wrecked, Identity Theft,* and *Followers*—and has worked as an editor at *Redbook* and *Cosmo.* Currently Anna is working on her "grown-up" novel. A graduate of Barnard College, she sort of lives in Brooklyn but makes it a priority to travel and explore new places whenever she gets a chance.

AMY DRESNER is an L.A. native who graduated magna cum laude from Emerson College, then moved to San

Francisco where she performed spoken word poetry at clubs and concerts. As a stand-up comic she's appeared at the Comedy Store, Laugh Factory, BATS Improv Theatre, and many clubs you'd be ashamed to be at. She's been published in *Salon, AlterNet, After Party Chat,* and more; completed a screenplay about celebrity rehab; and is working on her first novel about the story of a life going nowhere.

SAMANTHA DUNN is the author of the novel *Failing Paris* and the memoirs *Not by Accident: Reconstructing a Careless Life* and *Faith in Carlos Gomez.* Her essays are widely anthologized, including in the short story collection she coedited, *Women on the Edge: Writing from Los Angeles.* Her writing has been featured in many national publications, including *O, the Oprah Magazine, Ms., Glamour, InStyle, Shape,* and *Redbook.* An active member of PEN Center USA, she has served as advisor to its fellowship programs for developing writers: Emerging Voices and The Mark. She works as a staff writer at the *Orange County Register* and teaches memoir writing at the UCLA Extension Writers' Program, where she was named Instructor of the Year in 2011.

FIELDING EDLOW has had her plays developed/produced with Naked Angels, New York Stage & Film, PSNBC, Circle X Theatre Co., the New York

International Fringe Festival, the Hollywood Fringe Festival, and Comedy Central Stage. Her solo show, *Coke-Free J.A.P.*, won Backstage's Best of Fringe award at the FringeNYC festival before a four-month, sold-out run in L.A. Her full-length play, *The Something-Nothing*, was produced at the Lounge Theatre. She has performed in the live shows Sit 'n Spin, Show 'n Tell, and Afterbirth. Her newest solo play, *Sugar Daddy*, was performed at the Comedy Central Stage, and she's currently developing a comedy series for Showtime. She frequently does stand-up and lives in Los Angeles with her daughter and husband.

JANIE HADDAD TOMPKINS is a Los Angeles–based actress who was born in West Virginia and grew up in Charleston, South Carolina. Her credits include *Modern Family, Happy Endings*, and various *Funny or Die* shorts, and she is the voice of Margaret in Cartoon Network's Emmy-winning *Regular Show*. In addition to acting she loves podcasting, and she cohosts the charming *Janie & Aaron Does Hollywood* with her best friend, TV writer Aaron Ginsburg. She lives with her husband, the comedic genius Paul F. Tompkins, and yes, she does laugh all the time at home. You will see her soon as an ensemble member of a critically acclaimed television drama . . . because that's her dream and she won't give it up.

LAURA HOUSE is a comic, writer, and meditation teacher. She starred in MTV's *Austin Stories*, is a writer on CBS's *Mom*, and has also written for *Samantha Who?*, *Blue Collar TV*, *The George Lopez Show*, and *The Rosie O'Donnell Show* on OWN: Oprah Winfrey Network. You may have seen her on a campaign of Sprint commercials, opposite Natalie Portman as a hillbilly slut in *Where the Heart Is*, or hoarding M&M's from any number of craft service tables.

LAURA KRAFFT is a comedy writer, performer, and producer. She has worked on various television shows, including *The Colbert Report*, for which she won an Emmy. An alum of the Improv Olympic Chicago and Second City theaters, Krafft performs regularly around L.A. She's also written for *Vanity Fair*, *TAR* magazine, *New York Post*, and *Bust*.

JILLIAN LAUREN has an MFA in creative writing from Antioch University. She is the author of the novel *Pretty* and of the *New York Times*–bestselling memoir *Some Girls: My Life in a Harem*, both published by Plume/Penguin. Her writing has appeared in *The Paris Review*, *The New York Times*, *Vanity Fair*, *Los Angeles* magazine, *Flaunt* magazine, *Opium* magazine, Salon, *The Rumpus*, *The Nervous Breakdown*, and *The Moth* anthology, among others. She regularly blogs at jillianlauren.com, which was named a Top 100 Mom Blog of 2012 by *Babble*. She has performed at spoken word and storytelling events across the country. Jillian is married to musician Scott Shriner. They live in Los Angeles with their son.

VANESSA MARSHALL is a graduate of Princeton University with a masters in acting from NYU and is best known for her extensive voice-over career. As a stand-up comic and former "plus-size" model, she also created a successful one-woman show *Got Phat?*, which ran successfully in both L.A. and New York. She now performs regularly in her monthly storytelling event Show & Tell. Visit www.vanessamarshall.com for more details, as well as @VanMarshall for further musings.

JILL MORLEY wrote and performed the critically acclaimed play *True Confessions of a Go-Go Girl*. It was produced in Manhattan for five years, at San Francisco's Solo Mio Festival, at the Texas Fringe Festival, and at L.A.'s HBO Workspace, and it opened Women's History Month at NYU. *True Confessions* was published in the Women Playwrights series *The Best Plays of 1998* and was made into a Lifetime Movie of the Week. Jill's monologues and short stories are published in several anthologies. A contributing writer to *Village Voice, Fresh Yarn, New York Press,*

Penthouse, Inside Kung-Fu, Martial Arts and Combat Sports magazine, and *Gear* magazine, Jill also coproduced/cowrote two radio documentaries for *The World* and *This American Life.* Her documentary *Stripped* garnered good reviews from *The New York Times,* aired on Sundance Channel, and played theatrically in New York and Los Angeles. A late-in-life boxer, Jill documented her journey, as well as those of the talented women around her, in the documentary *Fight Like a Girl* (www.fightlikeagirlthemovie.com).

TAYLOR ORCI is a comedian who's contributed to *The Atlantic, Cosmopolitan,* and *New York* magazine. She's also appeared on Adult Swim, Comedy Central, and IFC. She used to work for NPR. Her comedy sketch, "Bitchy Resting Face," has over four million hits and became a thing people like Kate Moss talked about in interviews, which was like, wha? This morning Taylor ate spaghetti over the sink.

PAMELA RIBON is a TV writer, screenwriter, and best-selling novelist (*Why Girls Are Weird, Why Moms Are Weird, Going in Circles, You Take It From Here*). Pamela has adapted her popular novels for both film and television, and developed original series for ABC, ABC Family, Sony, and 20th Century Fox Productions. She is known as a pioneer in the blogging world with her successful website www.pamie.com. Her stage work has been showcased at the HBO U.S. Comedy Arts Festival and she created the accidental international scandal known as *Call Us Crazy: The Anne Heche Monologues*. She's currently writing a feature at Walt Disney Animation Studios and just released a comedic memoir of her awkward teen years called *Notes to Boys: And Other Things I Shouldn't Share in Public*.

SACHA Z. SCOBLIC is a writer and editor. She is the author of *Unwasted: My Lush Sobriety*, which is based on her popular essays for the *New York Times* blog *Proof: Alcohol and American Life*. Sacha is a 2012–2013 Rosalynn Carter Fellow for Mental Health Journalism through the Carter Center in Atlanta, Georgia. Sacha is a contributing editor at *The New Republic* and a frequent contributor to *The Huffington Post*. Formerly a senior editor at *Reader's Digest*, Sacha has written about everything from space camp to pulp fiction. She lives with her husband, Peter; son, Theodore; and terrier, SciFi, in Washington, DC.

RACHEL SHUKERT is the bestselling author of the books *Have You No Shame?: And Other Regrettable Stories, Everything Is Going to Be Great*, and most recently, the *Starstruck* series, a YA trilogy set in the golden age of Hollywood. Her writing has appeared in *Vanity Fair, New York* magazine's *Vulture, The Wall Street Journal, Salon, Slate, McSweeney's,* and *The Daily Beast,* and has been featured on National Public Radio and in numerous print anthologies. Shukert was born and raised in Omaha, Nebraska, and now lives in Los Angeles with her husband.

IRIS SMYLES has written for various publications including *BOMB, Nerve, Guernica,* and the *New York Press.* She was a humor columnist for *Splice Today,* edited the collection *The Capricious Critic,* and is the author of the novel *Iris Has Free Time.*

DIANA SPECHLER is the author of the novels *Who by Fire* and *Skinny,* as well as stories published in *The New York Times, The Wall Street Journal, GQ, Esquire, The Paris Review,* and elsewhere. She is the recipient of a number of writing awards, including a Steinbeck Fellowship from San Jose State University, a LABA Fellowship from the 14th Street Y, and a Sozopol Fiction Seminar fellowship. A six-time Moth StorySLAM winner, she has been featured on *The Moth* podcast and on NPR. She teaches writing in New York City and for the Stanford Continuing Studies Online Writer's Studio. Learn more at www.dianaspechler.com.

EMMA STRAUB is the author of the novel *Laura Lamont's Life in Pictures* and the short story collection *Other People We Married*. Her fiction and nonfiction have been published in *Vogue, Tin House, The New York Times, The Wall Street Journal*, and many other places. She lives in New York City, and will always love the New Kids on the Block.

CLAIRE TITELMAN is a comedian, actress, and writer based in Los Angeles. She was a semifinalist for the Andy Kaufman Award and performs stand-up and improv all over town as well as at festivals. She is a regular on the *Chelsea Lately* roundtable; a few of her other TV credits include *Parks and Recreation, New Girl, Veronica Mars,* and *Wilfred*. Her solo show, *Lemons Are for Emergencies Only*, was first produced in L.A. to rave reviews before its sold-out run at Edinburgh Festival Fringe in Scotland. She also performs with her comedy group Wet the Hippo.

CHELLIS YING has been published in Best Travel Writing, *Mental Floss*, and *Publishers Weekly* and was the runner-up for the 2010 Richard Bausch Short Story Prize. She received her MFA in writing at the University of San Francisco and a BA in literature at Kenyon College.

Acknowledgments

This book would not exist without the combined superpowers of my editor Dan Smetanka, who allowed me to pitch it to him during a book fair panel we were doing in 100-degree heat, and my agent Alexis Hurley. And the storytelling series the book is based on would not exist without co-producer extraordinaire Eric Martin, who balances out the ladies every month with talent, grace and sardonic humor to spare.

I'm also extremely grateful to so many others who have helped the True Tales wheel spin around, including Matt Ushkow, Todd Christansen, Deana Segretario and everyone else at The Mint and Joe Reynolds and everyone else at Mbar. Thank you as well to Jen Kuhn, Danny Jock, Christie Nittrouer, Justin Knox and

Kim Ohanneson, among so many other enthusiastic supporters.

Thanks as well to the Megan Fishmann, Liz Parker, and Emma Cofod triumvirate at Counterpoint/Soft Skull, Jen Heuer for designing the cover, Greg Behrendt for his fantastic forward, Eric Weis for his pinch-hit copy editing, and Gigi Levangie Grazer, Jackie Kashian, Annabelle Gurwitch, Jen Kirkman, Maria Bamford and the many other exceedingly talented women both in and out of this book who have appeared in the live show.